AT THE PEAK

HONG KONG BETWEEN THE WARS

To Glenna, Emily, Jessica and Joseph
For their love and forebearance.

AT THE PEAK

HONG KONG BETWEEN THE WARS

PAUL GILLINGHAM

First published 1983

ISBN 962 03 0218 4

Published by
MACMILLAN PUBLISHERS LIMITED
19/F, Warwick House, Taikoo Trading Estate,
28, Tong Chong Street, Quarry Bay,
Hong Kong.

Companies and representatives throughout the world

Printed in Hong Kong

CONTENTS

PREFACE

"The past is a foreign country; they do things differently there."

The Go-Between, *L.P. Hartley*

This book arose from a longing to discover what Hong Kong was like before it became the bustling, high-rise, sophisticated metropolis it is today. When I first arrived in 1975 many of the old buildings providing a link with the past were still standing, but in the course of the next eight years a good number succumbed one by one to demolition squads and the ambitions of property developers. Photographs from the old days only partly satisfied my curiosity: they revealed the physical shape of Hong Kong but little of how its people thought and felt.

The period between the two World Wars provided a convenient time structure within which to delve. While World War I had little direct impact on the colony, the Japanese invasion in 1941 brought to an end, at least for a time, a way of life which had undergone few changes since the last century. Two buildings, which have only recently been demolished, symbolised for me the changing nature of Hong Kong between the wars: the Repulse Bay Hotel, opened in 1920, reflected in its elegant low-rise porticoes the gracious living of an imperial past; the Hongkong Bank building, completed in 1935, represented in its modern high-rise exterior and art deco interior a rugged commercialism that looked to the future. I see the twenties and thirties as bridging the gap between the old Hong Kong and the new. Moreover, an added appeal of those two decades is that they are close enough to be recognisable, yet distant enough to reveal, as L.P. Hartley would have it, a foreign country where things *were* done differently.

Hong Kong before the last war was widely regarded as a rather sleepy place of no great significance in the British empire. But beneath the surface of what seemed to be a stable and comfortable colonial life there existed deep social and economic pressures and divisions. Across the border, China was suffering the spasms of civil and international wars which had painful repercussions on the life of the colony. Two general strikes, a year-long economic boycott and Chinese clamourings for an end to the "unequal treaties" by which Britain had gained Hong Kong cast doubt on Hong Kong's future as a British colony. *Laissez-faire* capitalism and limited government intervention in correcting the social evils of the time emphasised the divisions between rich and poor: those at the top of the social scale lived in luxury, while those at the bottom suffered appalling privations.

This book could never have been written without the help of others and I am particularly indebted to those who shared with me that portion of their lives spent in the Hong Kong of the twenties and thirties. My thanks go to Peggy Beard for allowing me full use of her superbly documented photograph collection and for spending many hours discussing the Peak life of her youth; Marjorie Angus for the use of her albums and the opportunity to talk at length about pre-war Kowloon; Amina el Arculli and her late sister Pat for their stories of life in Shatin when it was no more than a tiny settlement on the banks of the Shatin inlet; Bob Yates and

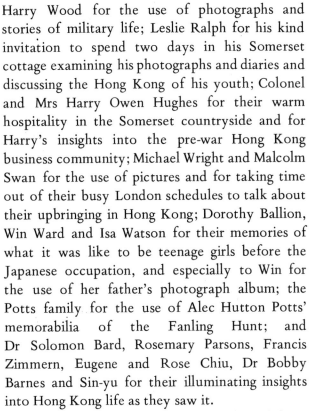

Harry Wood for the use of photographs and stories of military life; Leslie Ralph for his kind invitation to spend two days in his Somerset cottage examining his photographs and diaries and discussing the Hong Kong of his youth; Colonel and Mrs Harry Owen Hughes for their warm hospitality in the Somerset countryside and for Harry's insights into the pre-war Hong Kong business community; Michael Wright and Malcolm Swan for the use of pictures and for taking time out of their busy London schedules to talk about their upbringing in Hong Kong; Dorothy Ballion, Win Ward and Isa Watson for their memories of what it was like to be teenage girls before the Japanese occupation, and especially to Win for the use of her father's photograph album; the Potts family for the use of Alec Hutton Potts' memorabilia of the Fanling Hunt; and Dr Solomon Bard, Rosemary Parsons, Francis Zimmern, Eugene and Rose Chiu, Dr Bobby Barnes and Sin-yu for their illuminating insights into Hong Kong life as they saw it.

My thanks also go to others whose lives did not extend back into pre-war Hong Kong but whose help was equally valuable in the making of this book. Ian Diamond and Robyn McLean of the Hong Kong Public Records Office, who received the initial idea with great enthusiasm and guided me through the stages of documentary research with kindly professionalism; K.S. Au, who helped me sort through and copy some of the PRO's photographs; Elizabeth Sinn of the University of Hong Kong history workshop and Betty Chiu of Island School for their much needed advice on the Chinese perspective; Frederick Doe, general manager of Lane, Crawford, who put the company's archives at my disposal, and Stuart Muirhead, controller of group archives of the Hongkong and Shanghai Banking Corporation, who guided me through the myriad of bank documents and provided expert advice on banking matters; Sue Lambot and Sheila Foster for their help with typing and transcribing from recorded tape; Lesley Nelson, Francine Modderno and Howard Coats for their encouraging suggestions at times when the way forward seemed unclear; Rodney Bell and Sue Cope of Macmillan Publishers for their expert guidance on publishing matters; and Stephanie Holmes, my editor, for eliminating so many stylistic and grammatical errors from the original. Finally, very special thanks to my wife Glenna for assuming the role of both mother and father to our three children on those seemingly endless Saturdays when historical research took precedence over family life and to Shirley Woods, my typist, without whose determination under pressure and dedication in transforming pages of rough scribble into typed manuscript my jottings would never have reached the printing stage.

This book is not intended to be an exhaustive historical analysis. To attempt to compress the many facets of a complex community over a twenty-year period inevitably leads to simplification. I write for the general reader who wishes to know something of what Hong Kong was like in a bygone era. It is my hope that those living with the uncertainty of Hong Kong's future in the face of 1997 will gain some comfort from the fact that the community survived earlier threats to its existence and that those who lived through the twenties and thirties will catch glimpses, however fleeting, of the Hong Kong they once knew.

Paul Gillingham
London, 1983

1

PEACE CELEBRATIONS, 1919

Above, below, betwixt, between, we're competing with the moon,
Old Hong Kong's gay with bunting and light, not to mention Kowloon.

World War I ended, as far as Hong Kong was concerned, with a fizzle rather than a bang. A massive fireworks display which was to be the culmination of two days of celebrations to mark the coming of peace literally went off like a damp squib. The colony had paid out a sum of ten thousand dollars for the fireworks, and the firm which supplied them, Hitts, was given a roasting for having put on a poor show for the hundreds of thousands who gathered near the harbour to view the climax of the summer festivities in July 1919.

For two days the Crown colony of Hong Kong, tiny outpost of the still mighty British empire, was united like never before. The Great War of 1914-18 had barely ended and all communities in Hong Kong — European, Chinese, Eurasian, Portuguese, Indian and Japanese — celebrated the victory of Britain and her Allies over Germany in a riot of sound, light and colour.

All public buildings in Central were decked with thousands of red lanterns, which required putting up and dismantling miles of bamboo poles; triumphal and Chinese arches sprang up everywhere; spacious private houses were a blaze of lights; streets were draped with Allied flags; and every pillar and verandah was used to reflect the themes of "Victory", "Peace", "Long Live the Allies" and "United We Stand".

The perfect weather worked in favour of the celebrations as all available electric power had been exhausted in lighting up the outlines of major buildings, leaving thousands of others to rely on candle-light. The wide tree-lined streets of Kowloon were decked with lanterns and twenty-five triumphal arches dominated Salisbury and Nathan Roads. The event inspired some clever window dressing. Among the best was Messrs Komor and Komor, who had their three windows decorated in red, white and blue. The red window represented the Allies, with effigies of the British lion, Chinese ruler, American eagle, French cock and Japanese warrior; the blue window encased a bronze and ivory figure flanked by doves symbolising peace; and the white window, with the Canadian bear, Australian emu and Indian tiger represented the colonies.

Warships moored in the harbour were decked out in lights, as were the Star ferries shuttling backwards and forwards between them. A huge pink-lit dragon slung across a number of launches slipped past. From the air, shells exploded dropping British and American flags, parachutes, birds and fish.

On land, a motorcade of twenty-nine floats passed thousands of cheering onlookers. The loudest applause was for a trench-scene, "The Better 'Ole", perhaps because few in Hong Kong had experienced its reality. Mrs Grimble did well to stand still in the hot sun for an hour posing as a Red Cross nurse and supporting Mr Travis and Mr Kenyon as wounded soldiers. Their theme, "The Greatest Mother on Earth", also received a good round of applause, as did the boy dressed

> "Above, below, betwixt, between, we're competing with the moon,
> Old Hong Kong's gay with bunting and light, not to mention Kowloon.
>
> The cocktails flow, gin smashes foam, 'G' luck t' hic ye, old bean'
> Who did your bit to beat the Hun and lick him good and clean.
>
> The Hun has got it in the neck, he's crawling in the mud.
> He's a dirty, nasty thing, though at fighting no a dud.
>
> It's up to you to keep him there; he'll slither out of it if he dare,
> So Hong — hic — Kongites do your bit and keep the blighter there.

Central under the lights.

Statue Square.

2

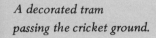

"Tonight we're having scenes of war, a' painted on the sky
By whizzing rockets, bursting bombs and Catherine wheels on high.

The Portuguese shout out 'Oh my !!!' The Chinese are in a whirl
And each young feller seizes his chance to squeeze the nearest girl.''

A decorated tram passing the cricket ground.

Decorations in Queensway

3

HMS Victory *and Lord Nelson.*

Float of naval cruiser.

up as Lord Nelson with his ship HMS *Victory*; Mr Ribeiro playing the heroic teenage gunner Jack Cornwall aboard HMS *Chester* in front of the sign "Hail British Youth, Follow Jack's Example"; and John Bull surrounded by colonial maidens dressed as "Our Little Bits".

For the Chinese population a mile-long fish-lantern procession, accompanied by six Chinese bands, weaved its way through the coolie districts from Happy Valley racecourse to Des Voeux Road Central. Eight hundred coolies carried lanterns, lit by one to twelve candles, in the shape of turtles, crocodiles, lobsters, sharks, lions, tigers, wolves and elephants with a one hundred yard long Great Dragon bringing up the rear.

On the Saturday afternoon a public naval and military display was held at the Cricket Club, followed by a private luncheon for the consuls of the Allied nations, hosted at the Hong Kong Hotel by the chairman of the General Committee of Peace Celebrations, Sir Paul Chater, and a reception for returned soldiers at Government House.

Milling crowds, swelled by thousands who came in from their villages in Kwangtung, were so great that pickpockets had a field day and the trams had to be suspended on Saturday night.

The celebrations were deemed by all, fireworks notwithstanding, to be a great success. It was remarked at the time that a unique aspect of the festivities was the "democracy of it all". People from every level of society, of all nationalities and races, whether from mansions high on the Peak, from homes in Kowloon, from the tenement hovels of the coolie districts or from huts in the New Territories, rubbed shoulders together in a seething mass of humanity. For many it was a unique experience, as inhibitions and business, social and racial considerations were discarded in the common goal of having a good time.

For some, however, the celebrations did nothing to relieve personal misery. In the midst of the festivities a twenty-five year old Chinese girl killed herself with an overdose of opium. A sixteen year old girl jumped into the harbour and only escaped death by the speedy action of a walla-walla. A Chinese man slit his throat with a razor. A twenty year old Chinese woman hanged herself in her tenement cubicle.

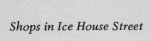
Shops in Ice House Street

Des Voeux Road from Jackson Road

Head Office, HKSBC

A week later dissatisfaction of a different kind exploded among the colony's poor, with a large-scale rice riot in the coolie districts, the first public disturbance the colony had seen for years.

Public order was quickly restored and Hong Kong settled down once again to its normal routine in what was generally recognised by casual visitors and those privileged enough to enjoy its gracious living as a kind of paradise on earth.

Like Somerset Maugham's heroine Kitty in *The Painted Veil*, the privileged few had "never paid anything but passing and somewhat contemptuous attention to the China in which fate had thrown her." Untouched by the physical presence of war and the consequences of the social and political upheavals which had shaken other societies to their roots, Hong Kong offered to people like Kitty the "facile existence of the luxurious East".

But to the coolie masses who flowed back and forth across the border with China to live in over-crowded hovels or, alternatively, the streets, there was no such luxury. For them, reality was more closely related to the suicides and the riots of that summer week in 1919 than to "squeezing the nearest girl". The lives of the coolie masses of Hong Kong came close to matching Thomas Hobbes' seventeenth-century view of human life as "nasty, brutish and short".

Across the border in China there raged a series of civil wars which would make their impact felt on Hong Kong whether people like Kitty cared or not. The rice riots of July 1919 were only a prelude to more serious social discontent which would be unleashed on the colony in two general strikes in the 1920s. Economic life was very nearly destroyed in a year-long boycott of Hong Kong's trade by the communist-inspired regime in Canton. Although no longer a "white man's grave", Europeans lived on a precipice beyond which plague still had the potential to strike and cholera raged annually. True, such dreaded diseases mainly affected the coolie masses, but it was tacitly understood that nobody was entirely immune. The twenties provided one set of anxieties, the thirties another. The Japanese invasion of China in 1937 brought the "yellow peril" within increasingly dangerous proximity of Hong Kong's borders until, finally, Japanese forces brought to an end the "facile existence of the luxurious East".

DIFFERENT WORLDS: PEOPLE AND PLACE

"My acquaintance with Hong Kong and with things Chinese now extends over a quarter of a century and nothing has been a cause to me of more anxiety throughout that period than the fact that the Chinese and the European communities of Hong Kong, although in daily contact with each other, nevertheless move in different worlds, neither having any real comprehension of the mode of life or ways of thought of the other. This is a most regrettable misunderstanding which retards the social, moral, intellectual and even the commercial and material progress of the colony."

Governor Cecil Clementi, 1926

"Are you married or do you live in Kowloon?"

Leslie Ralph, 1927

Hong Kong could not fail to impress visitors who sailed into the harbour for the first time. An Australian who came to see the peace celebrations wrote home in a vein similar to that of thousands of tourists who preceded him. "The noble façades of the waterfront and the dignity of the big white and grey mansions of the Mid-levels. Great and little steamers lying at anchor, a mass of junks with patched or torn sails lumbering along, a swarm of sampans, lighters and barges. In the centre handsome buildings, all providing cool and shaded colonnades, with shady trees and palms along the streets. Happy Valley looked especially beautiful with its golf course in the middle and hills rising steeply around, empty except for stately white mansions. From the ship you can see rickshaws moving from the centre to the valley along a tree-lined road."

For those who lived in those stately mansions and were able to play golf and travel by rickshaw, the reality was not very far removed from the illusion which the physical impression of the place could make on the untrained eye seeing it at a distance.

Pampered at home by an army of servants, working at a leisurely pace in well-fanned offices which had yet to face the pressures of instant teleprinters and the jet age, catered for by most forms of sport and homegrown entertainment, transported by sedan chair and rickshaw and socialised by membership of a variety of clubs, the expatriate in Hong Kong lived well. It did not matter all that much that some said Hong Kong was a sleepy little backwater lacking the brassy dynamism of Shanghai or the variety and high style of Bombay or Calcutta. The colony was a

7

pleasant enough place with plenty to do, little to worry about and enough creature comforts and leisure time to enjoy the good things in life.

"Hong Kong is not fashionable and never will be," said one well-heeled lady visitor who stepped off a P & O liner at Kowloon Wharf on her way around the world. To her, Hong Kong's weakness lay in the fact that, unlike London, Paris, New York, Malta, Simla, Biarritz or Mentone, it lacked a "season". Somerset Maugham was equally unimpressed by the colony's high society, which he lampooned in *The Painted Veil* but which nonetheless became a best-seller when it reached Hong Kong bookshops in 1925.

Nevertheless, to those who lived in the colony there were clearly defined social strata in which one's place was fixed according to race, nationality, position, accent and education. The Peak was a visible manifestation of class and position. On its upper reaches lived the taipans of the great hongs, their staff and leading civil servants. Only one Eurasian had a home there and he was probably the richest man in the colony. Other rich Chinese of the chief compradore class had spacious homes in the Mid-levels, chiefly on Robinson, Caine and Conduit Roads; the highest elevation they could possibly reach was May Road.

The better-off Japanese, who in the early twenties had earned some degree of acceptance by the British in Hong Kong, having defeated imperial Russia and joined the Allies in the war, had encroached as far as Macdonnell Road.

Austin Coates, in his book *Mountain of Light*, claims that between Macdonnell and May Roads lay a neutral zone where there lived "in the lower part, Portuguese, Jews, Armenians and Parsis, in the upper part — dreadful, but one had to concede it — 'dirty continentals', of whom the French were the most vigorous at nest-building and mountaineering. In what was socially the most triumphant of all their Asiatic aggressions, the French very nearly reached May Road. The French consul-general's fine old house on Old Peak Road shows to this day the point at which they were held; to avenge the loss of Calais, as it were." The fine old house he refers to has since been demolished, but his impishly put point is taken. Stratification did exist on the Peak and Coates' comment that " . . . from May Road upward to heaven was the exclusive preserve of those who gloried in the name of Briton" serves metaphorical if not literal truth.

Although Austin Coates did not turn his pen on the Americans, their number in the Hong Kong of 1921 had almost reached the five hundred mark, rather too high for some English tastes. Nevertheless, the Americans were at least preferable to the Germans. The small but lively German community had disgraced itself by its ties with the country which had dared to take up arms against Britain, and few were sorry to see the once thriving firms replaced after the war by American, Dutch and Japanese businesses.

Below the Peak lived the Chinese masses of the coolie class in dark, dirty, rat-infested, low-rise tenement buildings. The coolie districts of Western, Central and Eastern were grossly overcrowded, but the rising cost of land in the centre meant that the old wooden buildings which predominated there, as they still did in most Chinese residential areas, were steadily giving way to business premises.

The overcrowded conditions created such congestion that it was recognised in these years that the city would suffer without parks and green areas. "The city of Victoria is today entirely inadequately supplied with 'lungs'," said the Playing Fields Committee in 1930. It went on to make recommendations for open spaces "in order to preserve oases in what may one day become a world of bricks and mortar".

Across the harbour, Tsimshatsui offered spacious colonial houses amid wide tree-lined streets for Europeans whose social status and work as dockyard supervisors, marine engineers, police and prison officers and sea captains precluded them from living on the Peak. "Are you married or do you live in Kowloon?" asked Peakites, who thought any European residing in Kowloon was likely to be living with a Chinese woman, a situation which resulted in both

The Peninsula Hotel, 1939. The hotel was opened in 1928 by Hong Kong and Shanghai Hotels to serve travellers arriving by steamship and by train. There was not, in the early days, much to see or do in Tsimshatsui, but the Peninsula became the venue for the colony's major balls and social functions and helped to promote Kowloon as a socially acceptable area. It also established a reputation as one of the finest hotels in Asia.

partners being ostracised by their own communities. This damning condemnation of those who lived in Kowloon was, of course, rejected by residents such as Marjorie Angus, who lived in absolute respectability with her mother and father, a China coast sea captain, in a large house with a garden in Kimberley Road. "We didn't mix with Peakites. They looked down on us Kowloonites, but we considered we were just as good as them."

Kowloon residents often felt that the government was more concerned with the interests of Peakites rather than their own and in 1920 set up a Kowloon Residents' Association to press for a reservation similar to that on the Peak. The purpose of the reservation would be to protect Europeans and permanent residents of other races from land speculators and the hordes of immigrants from China. The association was at pains to emphasise that it had nothing to do with racial exclusiveness but was necessary to ensure a congestion-free area in order to preserve the health of foreigners living in a "hot and trying climate" and to offer protection in case of internal disorder.

The steady influx of Chinese across the border had indeed put pressure on Kowloon's housing situation, so that between 1919 and 1921 land prices in Tsimshatsui rose from two to seven dollars a square foot, higher than anywhere in the colony outside the business district of Central and the Peak. (Land in the island's hill districts cost twelve cents a square foot in 1921.) The opening of the Peninsula Hotel in 1928 did much to raise the social tone of Kowloon — as well as land prices there — and gave Kowloonites a classy rendezvous which rivalled the island's Hong Kong Hotel.

The New Territories was largely a wild untamed area roamed by tigers, wild boars and bandits. Six hundred or so villages supported a long-established rural population closely integrated into a traditional clan system which eked out a living from sea and soil. Similarly, the wild country of Hong Kong Island outside the built-up areas was interspersed with villages, especially along the coast. Shaukeiwan, Shek-O and Stanley were among the most lively, while Aberdeen was widely regarded by Europeans as "the most picturesque and charming village in the colony".

Hong Kong was very much a transitory place as far as the British were concerned. It was estimated in 1921 that the British population of slightly more than four thousand changed over almost completely in seven years, as most employees of big firms usually did one six-year tour and were then moved on to a posting elsewhere in Britain's far-flung empire.

The far greater Chinese population (ninety-nine per cent of the total) was equally transient. Less than twenty per cent of the Chinese people in Hong Kong and Kowloon were actually born in the colony; most came from villages in China, mainly men without their families. They worked in Hong Kong until they had built up meagre savings, then returned home. Such transience partly explains why many Chinese associations in the colony stressed their links with the homeland by incorporating the words "*Kiu Kong*", rather than "Hong Kong", in their titles (*kiu* means "overseas Chinese").

As late as 1939 there was a daily ebb and flow of about eight thousand people across the unrestricted border with China, although the thirties had seen a greater stabilisation in the local population as more and more workers brought their families with them and made Hong Kong their permanent home. The people of the New Territories were much more firmly rooted in the colony's soil, as nearly ninety per cent of the population was actually born there.

The boat people lived on the large numbers of sampans and junks in Hong Kong Harbour and off Stanley, Aberdeen and Shaukeiwan. Descended from the indigenous population of south China, their features and physique distinguished them from the Cantonese land population, by whom they were generally regarded as outcasts and with whom they rarely intermarried. The first to follow the trading fleet when it took refuge in Hong Kong Harbour before the island became British, the boat people could claim to represent the longest established community in the British Crown colony.

Indians, mostly originating from the Punjab and north-west frontier of British India, were largely employed in Hong Kong as policemen and watchmen. Although there were still a number of thriving Indian businessmen like the Arculli brothers, their commercial importance in the colony had declined since the abolition of trade in Indian opium. Sikh watchmen often had a sideline as professional money-lenders and the advent of the motor car in Hong Kong gave many of them work as chauffeurs. It was quite common for Indians to marry Chinese women, especially as second wives, and their offspring of mixed race worked mostly as clerks.

The once important Parsee community of Hong Kong was fast disappearing by the twenties and very few Parsee firms remained, although Sir Paul Chater retained a position of pre-eminence in society until his death in 1926. His home, Chater Hall on Conduit Road, was one of the most magnificent in the colony and his collection of works of art the envy of many wealthy Chinese and Europeans.

The closely knit, cohesive and thriving Portuguese community was descended from those of mixed race who had left Macau from the 1850s onwards, as Hong Kong replaced Macau as a trading entrepôt with China. Their language, a

Portuguese patois with traces of Hindustani, Malay, Japanese and Chinese, reflected the diverse cultures which had influenced Macau in its centuries as a major port on the Eastern trade route. In the Hong Kong of the twenties the "Portuguese" maintained their intermediate position between the Europeans and Chinese. They rarely married outside their own circle, had their own clubs, the Lusitano and Club de Recreo, were educated at La Salle and St Joseph's Colleges and worshipped in Catholic churches like St Teresa's and Rosary in Kowloon. Many worked in the professions and as clerks for major European firms, where their good knowledge of English gave them an advantage over the Chinese. The Hongkong and Shanghai Bank relied especially on the Portuguese to staff its banking hall, under British supervision, during the day; at night a second shift of Chinese staff employed by the bank's compradore would finish the accounting before the beginning of business the next day.

Another group which prided itself on its unique position between the British and Chinese was the Eurasian community. They were less obvious than the Portuguese, identifying more closely with the British or, as in the case of Sir Robert Ho-tung, with the Chinese. Not fully accepted by either, unless they were as prominent as Sir Robert, they developed strong interfamily ties and used their knowledge and insight into both cultures of East and West to good advantage in business and the professions. The long-established Eurasian families must be distinguished from those Europeans and Chinese couples who were more recently married; for them, acceptance by the Eurasians was as unlikely as by the communities from which they originated. "East is East and West is West and never the twain shall meet" was still a commonly held assumption in colonial Hong Kong, especially as far as romance was concerned.

Most of the foreign firms had strict, if unwritten rules about European employees becoming involved with Chinese of the opposite sex, and it was generally accepted that a European employee who openly developed a relationship with a Chinese girl risked his job and certainly the chance of promotion. Michael Wright, when he joined the Public Works Department as an architect in the thirties, had to sign a document to the effect that if he took a Chinese wife or concubine he was liable to dismissal. It was generally assumed that any Chinese girl with a European was a prostitute or "sleeping dictionary", although the ostensible reason for the ban on intermarriage was that it would create difficulties for the employee were he moved on. The taboo against interracial romance was not, of course, confined to Hong Kong. In 1930 the British Board of Film Censors forbade English actor John Longden from kissing the heroine, Chinese actress Anna May Wong, on screen in *Road to Dishonour* on the grounds that it would upset British audiences. It was all right for him to sit at her feet, kiss her hand and hold her in his arms, but not to kiss her on the lips, however demurely.

In government and the hongs there was a distinct level beyond which the Chinese, however able and well-qualified, could not rise. This caused resentment, especially among wealthy Chinese who had been educated at the best English schools and universities, and was paralleled by deep acrimony at their exclusion from the higher levels of the Peak and the Hong Kong Club. Governor Clementi saw the need for change if harmony were to be achieved between the races. His appointment of a Chinese, Chow Shou-son, to the Executive Council in 1926 and his revolutionary suggestion of an interracial club were attempts to bridge the gulf. In 1935 the acting colonial secretary, echoing the view of Governor Caldecott, went on record as saying, "Government has fully and frankly accepted the policy of replacing, wherever possible, European by Asiatic," but such resolve was slow in bearing fruit. It was not until after the war that the policy of localisation began to gather pace.

Chinese staff were, of course, employed by European firms, but not at high levels. The following memo from the manager of Lane,

MENU

Hors D'Oeuvres
Huitres au naturel   Caviare Croutes

Soup
Hare

Fish
Boiled Frazer Salmon and Egg Sauce

Entrees
Roast Quail
Pate de Foie Gras in Jelly

Joints
Roast Turkey
Braized York Ham and Port Wine Sauce
Roast Sirloin of Beef and Yorkshire Pudding
Saddle of Mutton

Iced Asparagus and Sauce a la Hollandaise

Roast Potatoes   Boiled Potatoes
Cauliflower   French Beans
Green Peas

Sweets
Plum Pudding and Brandy Sauce
Mince Pies   Fruit Jelly
Ice Cream and Wafers

Cheese   Fruit   Coffee

The mess, like the shop,
had its own formalities.
Christmas dinner for the bachelors,
with a few select ladies,
was a highly formal affair.

The Lane, Crawford
Mody Road, Kowloon,

*Grocery, wine and spirits department,
Lane, Crawford, Ice House Street, 1923.*

CAFE WISEMAN'S SPECIALITIES

All Cakes and Pastries are prepared by expert cooks in Café Wiseman's own Daylight Machine Bakery under the most scrupulously clean and hygienic conditions and expert European supervision. The ingredients used are of the very finest quality obtainable. Purity and excellence guaranteed. Post or telephone your orders if you cannot call.

Assorted Cakes, 5 cents each

Sponge Cake, Plain.	Elisen Cake with Butter Cream.
„ „ Iced.	Cream Puffs.
„ „ Layers.	„ Horns.
Shortbread, Round.	Napolean's Slices.
„ Iced.	Cream „
„ Long.	Macaroon „
Othello with Chocolate Icing.	Cocoanut „
Long and Round	Jam Rolls.
Othello with White or Pink	Madeira Cakes.
Icing, Long and Round.	And other Varieties which change
Chocolate Eclairs.	daily.
Dobush Cake with Butter Cream.	

English Cakes

Walnut Cake	80 cts. per lb.
Madeira „	60 „ „
Genoa „	$1.00 „
Coffee „	1.00 „
Russian Slice	1.00 „
Gatean small	60 „ „
„ large	1.00 „
Madeira Cake	60 cts. each.
Plum „	60 „ „
Seed „	60 „ „
Cherry „	80 „ „
Cocoanut Butter Cream Sponge ...	1.00 „
Chocolate Cake...	1.00 „
Melon „	1.00 „
Sacher „	1.00 „
Potato „	1.00 „
Sand „	60 cts „
Ginger „	60 „ „
Shortbread „	50 „ „
Sponge Cake	40 „ „

Delicious Home Made Chocolates $2.00 per lb. Fresh Every Morning.

'NAPIER JOHNSTONE'S' WHISKY

*Lane, Crawford catalogue, 1926. Café Wiseman in Lane,
Crawford was a favourite meeting place for tiffin. The
café specialised in cakes and pastries made under
European supervision.*

European shop assistant relaxing on the verandah of the Lane, Crawford mess, 1922.

Governor Sir Cecil Clementi opening the new Lane, Crawford store in Des Voeux Road, 17 August 1926.

Lane, Crawford ("Matsuzakaya") under Japanese occupation, 1943.

Crawford to his shop assistants in 1924 reveals something of the prevailing attitude of European management towards Chinese staff, as well as customer expectations. "The first customer to arrive in a department should be served by the Number One of that department. Subsequent customers should be served by the European assistants until all are engaged, when Chinese and other Asiatics will be brought forward to serve. The Number One in each department should, whenever possible, make a point of speaking to the customers being served by juniors or Asiatic salesmen, in order to ensure that such customers are receiving, or have received, the attention and satisfaction to which they are entitled."

The wide gulf separating Europeans, and especially the British, from the Chinese population was very much a legacy of the British empire. Hong Kong's Reverend Copley Moyle could, in 1919, preach a sermon on the "white man's burden" without blinking an eyelid. The ethos of Kiplingesque superiority remained strong between the wars, for the British empire still ruled as large a part of the earth's surface as it had in its late-Victorian heyday and its leaders were unaware that the Ghandian stirrings against it would lead to its eventual demise. Old traditions die hard, and within Britain itself the social gulf separating members of the upper-class establishment from the London docker was as wide as that which separated them from Indians, Chinese and other races in their empire.

A sense of racial superiority came as easily to the British as it did to the Chinese, rooted as the latter were in the tradition of the Middle Kingdom; China saw herself as midway between heaven and earth and her rulers were said to exercise power by virtue of the mandate of heaven. The British in Hong Kong could, moreover, point to China's recent history: the impotence of the late Manchu rulers; the failure of the 1911 Revolution to achieve the goals laid down by Sun Yat-sen; the misrule and corruption of the warlord era; the inability of Chiang Kai-shek to fully unite the country or raise its general standard of living — all were evidence for many

that the Chinese were an inferior race, incapable of keeping their own house in order.

Those who held such views were not necessarily racial bigots but happened to reflect the thinking of their time. A kindly humanitarian like Gilbert Baker, who worked in the church in Canton in the 1930s recognised, in visits to Hong Kong, that "the prevalent feeling was that the Chinese were a rather hopeless people, especially as China itself was in a mess".

It was not surprising that the University of Hong Kong, opened in 1912, was seen as fulfilling the role of "a great British lighthouse built upon the most prominent rock of the China coast in the darkest age of Asia", even if it was conceded in the thirties that the lighthouse was badly in need of proper and efficient lighting and was only dimly reflecting the benefits of British civilisation.

In Hong Kong the only contact most Europeans had with Chinese people was in the form of domestic staff. There was then virtually no Chinese middle class with whom they could work on equal terms, while the few rich Chinese kept very much to themselves and the Chinese visible on the streets were mainly of the coolie class.

The wide social and economic gulf between the races created distrust on both sides. During the taking of the decennial census in 1921, a rumour circulated in coolie districts to the effect that the government intended building a bridge across the harbour which would rest on ninety-nine piers filled with the bodies of three hundred Chinese children and an unspecified number of pregnant women. It was widely believed that the purpose of the census was to enable the government to make a suitable choice of persons. Census officials had great difficulty in making correct returns, especially in Wanchai and Shaukeiwan where children were locked up for days until the Chinese press was encouraged to scotch the rumours.

If the Chinese distrusted the motives of the British, the British in turn questioned the loyalty of the Chinese. The two general strikes of the early twenties were proof to many that in times of crisis the local population could not be relied upon. Following the 1925 strike Chinese police-men were disarmed, and a burning question in the thirties, especially after the Japanese invasion of China, was whether to allow local Chinese to join the Hong Kong Volunteers. However, the growing Japanese threat and the need for Chinese support in the event of an attack on Hong Kong won the day and led to the inclusion of a Chinese company in the Volunteers.

The laws of Hong Kong came down harshly on Chinese who threatened the European way of life, as the record of punishment for petty crimes between the wars suggests: twelve months' hard labour and eighteen strokes of the birch for stealing a handbag with twenty-four dollars in it from a European woman in Des Voeux Road; twelve months' hard labour and twenty-four strokes of the birch for ripping gold earrings off an amah walking down Peak Road (she happened to work for the acting manager of the Hongkong and Shanghai Bank); six months in gaol and four hours in the stocks for stealing iron railings from houses in the Bowen Road area; three months' hard labour for snatching a European's felt hat as he rode in a rickshaw along the Praya.

The population of Hong Kong at the beginning of the twenties was officially estimated at just over 625,000, less than 13,000 of whom were non-Chinese. This figure from the 1921 census was later described as wildly inaccurate by the 1924 government committee on opium. Their reasoning was most bizarre. They cited the evidence of a nightsoil contractor who sold the bulk of Hong Kong's faeces for mulberry growing. Working from the 1921 census figure and allowing that the average person produced three taels of nightsoil a day, he estimated that his total haul would be 1,275 piculs daily. Not wishing to take chances, he reduced the expected take to 1,100 piculs to allow for wastage through water closets and boat people and tendered accordingly. To his great surprise the amount of nightsoil he actually collected was close to 2,500 piculs (or four million taels), leading him and the opium commission to conclude, by simply dividing the three taels a head into the total, that the 1921 population of Hong Kong was more in the region of 1,300,000.

This charge of inaccuracy was not, of course, one which the census office could afford to ignore. Accordingly, they devoted a section of their 1931 census report to the "fable" of the nightsoil contractor of 1921, whose conclusion they criticised on the basis that three taels per person per day was too low in view of the population's staple diet of rice, which left a bulky and heavy residue. They quoted a book, *Sanitation in War*, by Lieutenant-Colonel L.S. Lelean, in which the author states that the average person gets rid of four and a half ounces of faeces and five ounces of urine a day, twice as much as the contractor's figure. Give or take an ounce or two, the census officials felt that eight ounces (or six taels) per person a day was about right, just enough for them to triumphantly conclude that the amount of nightsoil collected by the contractor in 1921 proved that their original figure of 625,000 people in Hong Kong was correct after all. The census officials had, as far as they were concerned, proved their point, even if they had to admit that the subject was somewhat unusual for a census report.

3

THE PEAK

Before she arose to the Peak
Matilda was timid and meek,
But now she offends
Her Bowen Road friends
With a smile that is cutting and bleak.

There was no doubt about it: elevation to the Peak above May Road meant a rise in social status in a world in which precedence and degree had not yet suffered the onslaughts of egalitarianism. It seemed natural that the well-bred English should live on a level which placed them above other human beings.

Many compared the Peak to Simla, India's hill station north of Delhi, where the viceroy and the English social set escaped the rigours of the hot season below. As in Simla, those living on the Peak were cut off from the rest of the population by height, distance and social barriers. Like Matilda in the 1930 poem quoted above, Peakites lived in a world of their own. As Peggy Beard remembers from her life there in the twenties, "If you lived at the Peak you lived at the Peak. Everybody seemed to know everybody. You didn't know anybody else. Height didn't really matter, but if you lived at May Road it wasn't quite so good. I'd never even heard of Conduit Road." Her father, a partner in the architectural firm of Palmer and Turner, designed and built the family home, 28 The Peak. Perched on Lugard Road, it was close to the pinnacle of the mountain, on the very top of which stood the governor's summer residence.

Han Su-yin, in her novel *A Many Splendoured Thing*, was rather more cutting: "They are afraid to lose caste within the narrow circle to which they are confined by the scope of their interests; to be rejected from the social herd for any peculiarity of thought; to lose in the struggle for conformity up the nicely graduated steps of the island hierarchy. Their aim is to attain that chimerical upper stratum of birth and financial security which only exists in the English middle-class mind, but which, in the colony, is still so doubtfully symbolised by that eminence called THE PEAK."

Climbing up the graduated steps of the island hierarchy involved not only securing a foothold on the Peak, getting invited to Government House, being given an overdraft at the Hongkong and Shanghai Bank and considered for membership of the Hong Kong Club, but also having a pew close to the altar in St John's Cathedral. Cathedral pews could be rented by the year and this entitled the holder to a name plaque and the sole right to use it. After World War I it was felt by many that social distinctions in church did not accord with peacetime feelings, after so many people of different classes had shared the sacrifices and hardship of war.

The matter came to a head in 1915 when a newly arrived territorial battalion of the King's Shropshire Light Infantry needed seats in the cathedral for their Sunday church parades. Pew-holders were asked if all places could be declared free three minutes before the morning service at eleven o'clock. They agreed, with some degree of reluctance on the part of a few. At the 1917

The newlyweds, Peggy and Kenneth Beard,
St John's Cathedral, 18 December 1928.

Groom and attendants: (From left)
Eileen de Biere; Reta Hazeland;
Lieut. Kenneth Beard, RN;
Lieut. C.G. Trencham, RN;
Eileen Stubbings; Dorothea Bewley.

The acting governor of Hong Kong,
Mr W.T. Southorn, and his wife
arrive for the ceremony.

Matelots with firecrackers
at the reception,
Volunteer headquarters.

19

annual pew-holders' meeting one member made the radical suggestion that the renting of pews be abolished. He was voted down in favour of a motion that all seats be declared free a full five minutes before the start of morning service, but when a second special meeting was called to confirm the new arrangement it was turned down, although a compromise was reached with a decision to free all pews at evensong. In the following year pew-holders went even further in their concession to democracy when they agreed that seats would be freed at matins after the bell had stopped tolling.

By the late twenties feeling had swung behind the abolitionists and in 1928 the renting of pews in St John's Cathedral was finally brought to an end. The twenties were a decade of modernisation in other areas for the cathedral. 1921 saw the replacement of hand-operated punkahs by electric fans, and 1924 the spending of the huge sum of fourteen thousand dollars on refurbishing the organ, which had cracked in the tropical heat. The cathedral brought out an English organ expert to rebuild it, but as he had little idea of the rigours of the tropical climate, the organ needed doing again ten years later.

The Peak area was the most beautiful in Hong Kong. A publicity booklet of 1924 described it as having "the appearance of public grounds, the roads leading from one level to another being lined with palms, ferns and flowers" and compared it to the Highlands of Scotland with European residences "perched like eagles' eyries" among "granite peaks and frowning precipices". The Peak district had been made accessible with the opening of the Peak Tram in the 1880s and had become such a desirable residential area that a second Peak Tram was planned to go up the Glenealy ravine. The Peak had its own hotel, beside the upper terminus of the Peak Tram, its own hospital, its own church, its own club and a large military barracks which could offer it protection.

Residents belonged to a Peak Residents' Association, and English governesses had to have a special permit to live on the Peak. No coolie bearing a load could travel on the Peak Tram which meant, in the days before the opening of Stubbs Road made it accessible by motor car, that they had to walk up Old Peak Road lugging coal, ice, luggage, provisions and building materials on their shoulders.

At various points on the Peak there were "halts" which were used by load-bearing coolies for shelter and rest. In 1921 a Reverend Wells spent the day in one of them to gather evidence on working conditions for a commission on child labour in Hong Kong. In his report, the Reverend wrote of one six year old boy who, with his widowed mother, had started out at five o'clock that morning after a meagre breakfast. He had picked up two twenty-two catty (twenty-nine pound) loads of coal at Central market, which was then on the seafront or Praya, and was lugging them up to a house on the Peak. His technique was to move each load a certain distance before going back for the other one. His work would be over at 5.00 p.m. He carried fifty-eight pounds of coal up the Peak six days a week. His pay for such Herculean labour? Eight cents a day.

The boy's mother carried nearly three times as much (150 catties) for a daily wage of twenty-seven cents. There were some men in the same hut and they told Reverend Wells that their pay was eighteen cents per one hundred catties (133 pounds) of coal and that they carried two such loads up the Peak, using the same method as the boy, for a daily wage of thirty-six cents. It was due to the efforts of people like these that taipans were able to sit snugly beside their Peak coal fires waxing eloquent on such themes as the "white man's burden".

No Chinese, except for domestic staff, were allowed to live on the Peak before the end of World War II. The only exception was Hong Kong's first millionaire, Sir Robert Ho-tung, whose long white beard and the traditional Chinese gown he habitually wore gave him a mandarin-like appearance. Only his sparkling blue eyes betrayed his Eurasian origins.

The "grand old man of Hong Kong" had won

Sir Robert Ho-tung's Peak residence, The Falls, 1937.

the right to live on the Peak through his wealth and influence. He was awarded the first knighthood given to a Eurasian or Chinese in 1915. Illness had forced his retirement as Jardine's head compradore in 1898, and by the interwar years he had become something of an eccentric. One of his daughters, Irene Cheng, said that if she or any of her seven sisters and four brothers wanted to see their father, they would have to ask for an appointment, which normally lasted fifteen minutes. Alternatively, they wrote him a memo, to which he sent a written reply typed by his secretary.

In 1906 Sir Robert bought three houses on the Peak, The Chalet, Dunford and The Neuk, and later had a palatial mansion, The Falls, built complete with a swimming pool filled by the natural waterfall which gave the mansion its name. Having a number of houses gave Sir Robert the opportunity to live separately from his two wives and twelve children (one son was adopted). The Peak homes were not, however, the only houses owned by Sir Robert Ho-tung. He also had a mansion in Seymour Road, Idlewild; Ho-tung House in the city, with offices and apartments; a farm in the New Territories; houses in Macau, Shanghai and the beach resort of Tsingtao; and a large house near London's Kew Gardens complete with tennis court and bedrooms with bathrooms attached, a rarity in England in 1932. In addition he had several boats, one of them anchored off the Praya in Central to which he walked daily from his office for lunch on board.

In spite of such fabulous wealth, Sir Robert and

his family were never entirely accepted by taipan families on the Peak. One of his daughters, Jean Gittins, who claims to have been the first Eurasian to be born on the Peak, wrote in her autobiography, *Eastern Windows — Western Skies*, that other children "might suddenly refuse to play with us or they might tell us that we should not be living on the Peak".

Whatever the feelings of Europeans towards the Ho-tungs, many of them appreciated the services of one of the family's servants, a blind masseuse named Lin Goo. Having joined the family from Canton in 1932 to ease Lady Clara Ho-tung's rheumatism, she was employed, after Lady Clara's death, as Sir Robert's night nurse at The Falls. This remarkable woman, who was able to recite the *Four Books* of the Confucian classics by heart, made enough extra money massaging people on the Peak to buy two flats of her own in Hong Kong after the war.

It was claimed at the time that reserving the Peak for Europeans had nothing to do with racial discrimination. The purpose of the reservation was "to provide a congestion-free area which would preserve the health of foreigners living in a hot and trying climate and which, in times of strike or internal disorder, would afford some protection". Michael Wright believes that the racial exclusiveness of the Peak arose out of a genuine fear of disease and the belief that, if Chinese were allowed to live there, they would start building Chinese-style tenement houses which, on the lower levels, were notoriously filthy.

The Peak's uncongested environment protected its denizens from the diseases which ravaged the coolie masses below. The Peak even became sufficiently mosquito-free by the late thirties to allow residents to dispense with that domestic article so essential to foreigners living in the Orient, the mosquito curtain.

A great advantage of the Peak was that, in the days before air-conditioning, it was five or six degrees cooler than the lower levels at night. As people dressed more formally then, even on casual occasions, the cooler air in summer was welcome. Even so, Peggy Beard remembers the family having a punkah before electric fans came in. "Father even had a punkah in his office at Palmer and Turner — a little boy sitting out on the verandah of his office in Alexandra House, with his string. We had a punkah in our dining room at Lugard Road. He would be sitting there and then he'd fall asleep and Father would shout at him: 'Wake up! Get on with it!' They were lovely things as they went right across the room and you got a really good breeze."

The benefit of losing a few degrees in the summer, however, was offset by the uncomfortable chilliness of the winter, when the barometer could plunge dramatically. Peakites fortified themselves against the cold with roaring fires and stiffer drinks. The *Hongkong Telegraph* reported in 1932, "A local taipan swears he's seen ice on the Peak. We've often heard this about cocktail time."

Coping with mildew was always a problem for Peakites. Fur coats could be stored during the hot season in a refrigerated room on the top of the Dairy Farm building in Wyndham Street and in every Peak residence there was a large drying room with a coke stove in it, which kept the Peak fire station busy. Before flush toilets, all Peak residences had dry latrines or "thunderboxes", as the locals called them. Coolies came round every day to collect the nightsoil, which was loaded on to barges and dumped into the sea off Lantau, or sold off to a contractor who in turn sold it to farmers as fertiliser. In spite of no mains drainage, however, the Peak was in many ways very modern. Michael Wright recalls that his parents' house on Coombe Road had a telephone and electric lights before 1920. "When I went to stay with my grandmother in England, she was on gas and nobody in her area had a telephone. We were 172 The Peak and I remember that our telephone number was 1172."

Leslie Ralph remembers the Union Insurance mess on the Peak having a big "Soochow bathtub". The correct way to have a bath was to stand beside the tub and splash yourself from a bowl. "To get into the tub was a criminal offence.

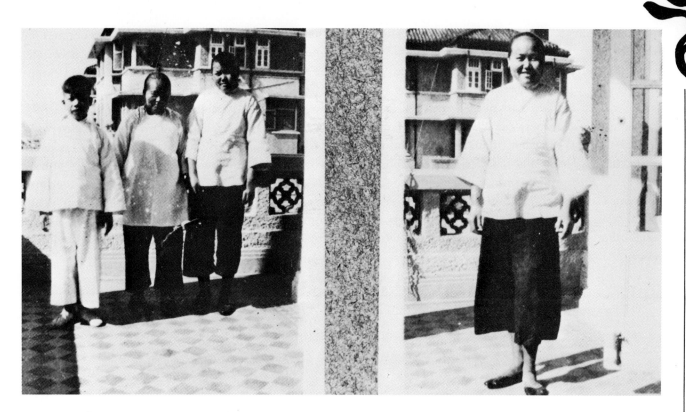

Peggy Beard's servants, 298 Prince Edward Road, Kowloon, 1932. As a newly married couple, Peggy and Kenneth Beard had three servants: a boy who served at table, a wash amah and an all-purpose amah.

People just out from home were inclined to get in! Water wasn't all that plentiful so it was a way of saving it. The same bath water would do for everyone."

All Peak families had a large staff of servants. The Kotewalls, an eminent, Mid-levels Eurasian family, had twenty-six servants, but this was the exception rather than the rule. Labour was cheap and times for the ordinary Chinese were hard, so servants were inexpensive and plentiful. Peggy Beard's parents had a cook, a market coolie, a Number One boy, a Number Two boy, a wash amah, a *fa-wong* (gardener) and four chair coolies to carry the family's two sedan chairs. As an indication of their precedence in the household, the most valued member, the cook, was paid thirty dollars a month, the Number One boy twenty-five and the others twenty. The governess, whom they had brought out from England to look after Peggy's younger sister, received forty dollars as she was British and, even though a servant, a cut above the rest of the household.

The ten servants lived in rooms in the basement, although the English governess had her own room next to the baby's.

Michael Wright's parents had a similar sized household, which they could well afford in the early twenties. Seven servants costing less than a hundred dollars a month represented about a tenth of the monthly family income. When he returned to Hong Kong in 1938 as a Public Works Department architect and lived with two other bachelors, they shared a cook boy, a wash amah and a coolie who took the dog for a walk. The cook boy received thirty dollars a month, the amah eighteen and the coolie twelve. "Hong Kong was an incredibly cheap place when I went out in 1938." With so many servants, the European family had hardly to lift a finger and it was no wonder topees could be whitened daily.

There was a special uniform for servants. Houseboys and amahs, male and female, wore black trousers and white jackets. Drivers wore white suits, socks and shoes. Servants were rarely referred to by name, but as "Boy" (even if he were in his sixties) or "Amah", and the employers were "Master" and "Missie". Education was very limited for the Chinese in Hong Kong and servants, like coolies, had never learned English, so communication between "Boy" and "Master" or "Missie" was in pidgin. Language was reduced to its simplest form and pidgin was not only used between Europeans and Chinese, but also between Cantonese and Chinese from other areas. If the servants in Peggy Beard's household started squabbling in their quarters, her mother would

that had got soggy with the wet three times in one night." If there were dancing, music would be provided by gramophone records or by a three-piece Filipino band which could be hired for ten dollars for the evening.

Leslie Ralph lived in the Union Insurance mess with a number of other young bachelors who worked for the company at a large house, Hillcrest, 114 The Peak. "Our mess was noted for its New Year's Eve parties and there was great competition among the girls to come to it. We converted Hillcrest at one time into a medieval

Peak fancy dress party, 1927. Fancy dress was taken seriously in those days: many people had their costumes especially tailored, although this particular party was less elaborate than most.

shout at them, "Too muchy bubbery!" In pidgin "You understand?" became "You savvy?"; "Go upstairs and make the beds" became "Go topside and fixee beds."

A major factor of Peak life was the dinner party, with people seated at assigned places. Dinner was a full seven courses and was served by the Number One and Number Two boys with a white cloth over their arms to each guest in turn. Men wore dinner jackets and ladies long dresses. Gloves for the ladies were optional. Michael Wright remembers wearing a dinner jacket three or four times a week to private dinner parties, and always a stiff collar, even in summer. "I remember changing butterfly collars

castle. We had a portcullis on the front door, with beefeaters on either side. Most costumes were from the amateur dramatic society. My room was made into a public house, with sawdust on the floor. I was mine host in knee breeches and all the guests wore medieval clothes."

The business of dressing up beforehand was taken very seriously. The Raven sisters, Dorothy and Winifred, consulted books on costume design and, having decided who or what they would go as, invariably went to the tailors to have their costumes specially made.

Servants in the messes had a lot to put up with. Their bachelor "Masters", not long out of public school or university, tended to see life outside the

24

office routine as an extension of their student days. According to Leslie Ralph, "We would invite the Jardine's mess for games of poker – our mess against theirs. To start with, our visitors had to run through a barrage of flour and soot. There was a sense of rivalry between the two messes. We would sometimes raid each other's messes and steal something as a trophy."

Such pranks were an integral part of a young fellow's life in pre-war Hong Kong. It was all regarded as good fun, a means of letting off steam. "Poor old Queen Victoria in Statue Square. She was always in trouble after a big party, with someone putting a straw hat or a bowler on her crown. On one occasion somebody hauled a domestic utensil up the flagstaff of Flagstaff House and cut the halyards so they couldn't get it down. In those days I used to think it was funny. Today it would be regarded as vandalism."

Conversation on the Peak was mostly limited to the matters of everyday living. Servants, gossip and business predominated, as they did in conversations throughout the empire. A young journalist working for the *Overland China Mail* recorded the following conversation at the Peak Club in the winter of 1931. "Did you know that Mrs —— had tea with Mr —— the other day? Miss —— slapped Mr —— 's face and said, 'Oh, yew are a one, yew are.' Mrs —— was seen arm in arm with a soldier on Mount Kellet Road. Mr —— is on the verge of bankruptcy, didn't you know? Mr —— wasn't at Oxford at all and spent the night in the police cells last week. Mrs —— said to her husband on the Peak Tram the other day, 'I hope you've washed your face, deah.' Mr —— won't retire until he gets a title. Mr —— never shaves on Sundays and doesn't go out until after dark. Miss —— locks her bedroom door every night at the Peak Hotel."

Married women were the most vulnerable to boredom, with children away at boarding school and a team of servants to cover every conceivable job in the home. They were not encouraged by husbands or by society to get involved in charity work, nor were they easily able to find jobs. The

The Author, in 1893. (inset 1925)
Arrived in Hongkong 14th March, 1879.

Mr R.C. Hurley, 1925.

only support they had was one another, so endless bridge sessions at the Peak Club were, for many, the only escape from depression. For those who could not bear the tedium of life in Hong Kong, there was always the option of returning to England to be close to their children's boarding school (and their mothers) or, like the heroine in *The Painted Veil*, surreptitiously meeting a lover in the back room of a seedy opium shop in Cat Street.

There was considerable social pressure to conform. Occasionally, though, the Peak did throw up the odd eccentric like old Mr Belilios, who kept a camel in the grounds of his Peak residence at the turn of the century. In the 1920s there lived on Coombe Road a Mr Hurley whom Michael Wright remembers well. "He had a motorless motor car, like a child's motor car except that it didn't have pedals, but was big enough to take a full-grown man. Every morning he walked down

The Peak Hotel, 1930. The hotel was taken over by Hong Kong and Shanghai Hotels in 1922 from a Mr Findlay Smith, who opened it in 1908. Smith had been one of the promoters of the Peak Tram in the 1880s. He later obtained a concession from the government to build a rival tramway up the Glenealy ravine but was bought out by the Peak Tramways Company.

to the office in Victoria, as most people did in those days, followed at a respectful distance by his market coolie carrying a change of clothes. After work he would take the Peak Tram up to the Barker Road station, where he was met by a coolie with his motorless motor car. The coolie, who had pushed it all the way up to the station, gave him a gentle shove and Mr Hurley would free-wheel all the way home. One day he was speeding past the stone seat at the junction of Barker and Coombe Roads, where amahs congregated and the children in their charge played, when he knocked one of the kids over. The child survived, but all

hell was let loose and the commissioner of police personally ordered him not to 'drive' his car again."

The Peak Hotel was home for a number of elderly residents who wanted to live permanently "topside" because they liked the view, the bracing air and the proximity of the tram. They were well looked after by a staff supervised by a formidable but kindly housekeeper who was the mother of one of Peggy Beard's bridesmaids, Eileen Stubbings. Marjorie Angus and her friends usually stopped off at the hotel for tea and crumpets after a bracing winter walk round the

Come to the Peak. Ha! Ha!

Some hyperaesthetics scream out to suppress
Cracker-firing; while others direct their rebukes
At aeronaut zoomers. Some try to redress
The false notes of gramophones, saxophones, ukes,
My bête noire is that oiseau de mauvais augure
Who advises in accents impeccably pure,
"Come to the Peak. Ha! Ha!"

If my Sunday is blank, in my mid-level flat
For an afternoon's nap, I sometimes extend.
I toss and I turn, try this side and that,
But repose is a mood that I can't comprehend.
"Oh is there a breeze in this island!" I cry
And that fiend of a bird makes the scoffing reply,
"Come to the Peak. Ha! Ha!"

And when I'm invited to tennis up there,
And climb on a tramseat at Kennedy Road,
Should it chance that a dripping wet fog fills the air
And the universe feels like a vault for a toad,
As I take my last mouthful of dry atmosphere
The bird on the hillside lets loose a grim jeer —
"Come to the Peak. Ha! Ha!"

I play golf at Fanling on a dazzling day,
When the ball is a basilisk's eye in the grass.
If I'd kept my eye on't, I venture say
T'would have blasted my eyesight.
I was out of my class.
I foozled my putts; sclaffed shots off the tee.
And each time I swore, the bird echoed with glee,
"Come to the Peak. Ha! Ha!"

In a thunderstorm once on Dairy Farm Hill
I sailed with my car, even backed in reverse.
Get out and get soaked? Or wait here until
The tropical storm clouds of summer disperse?
That was the question I asked of the night.
That bird in the coarse grass replied with delight,
"Come to the Peak. Ha! Ha!"

From Stanley or Shek-O, to Castle Peak Bay,
Cheung Chau to High West or the Taimoshan crags,
Be you outdoors or indoors, you can't get away
From this bird which incessantly, tirelessly brags.
Who first was the wretch with the disarranged brain
That instructed a bird to proclaim the refrain
"Come to the Peak. Ha! Ha!"

Robert Simpson 1933

top of the Peak. "It was the only place in Hong Kong where you could get fresh, hot crumpets and they used to serve them in a big, silver dish. In the lounge there were two huge fireplaces at each end. It was lovely to sink back in a deep sofa with the fires blazing and have tea and crumpets served to you in style."

In spite of such good service, business for the hotel, run by Hong Kong and Shanghai Hotels, was never as good as for the company's other hotels, the Hong Kong Hotel, the Peninsula and the Repulse Bay Hotel, and on 1 September 1936 the Peak Hotel closed its doors for the last time.

A major aspect of social etiquette practised in Hong Kong and throughout the British empire was cardcalling. The first thing a new arrival did in Hong Kong was to get cards printed with his name and the government department, hong or bank he worked for. He would then set out on foot to the houses of the Peak, dropping off his cards at boxes at the entrance to Peak residences to announce his arrival in Hong Kong. The practice was such a fundamental part of Peak life that Lady Bella Southorn, wife of the chief secretary, devoted a whole chapter to it in her book, *Under the Mosquito Curtain*. Lady Southorn saw it as an essential difference between East and West: "The East has a box and the West doesn't."

The problem for those who had just arrived in Hong Kong was making friends and meeting people, and this was where cardcalling came in. Social etiquette demanded that you did things properly, so dropping your card off was a means of announcing who you were and giving people the opportunity to invite you to dinner if they liked the sound of you or felt obliged to do so as you were in a similar line of business.

Eric Himsworth, who came out to Hong Kong as a young government cadet in 1928, looks back on the practice with some cynicism. "On my first free day after arriving in Hong Kong, I was taken on a walking tour of Peak residences by a senior colleague, having already had printed a box of a hundred cards for one dollar. It was a hard day's work and the colleague told me that eighty per cent would ignore me, fifteen per cent would send me their own card in return and five per cent might, if I was lucky, invite me to dinner. In fact, about two per cent did."

The boxes which received the cards had a sliding device on them with the words "In" and "Out", fixed permanently at "Out" as a form of protection against unwelcome visitors. Lady Southorn recalled some of the stories circulating the Peak about the box and cardcalling. A drunken taipan on his way home at three in the morning passed a box announcing "Mrs Jarvis NOT AT HOME" and dropped in a message with the words, "Well, you damned well ought to be." Up-and-coming Jardine executive Hamish McTavish had spent a day putting cards in boxes and being greeted by nobody. Finally trudging up the steep path leading to the house of a junior partner, he saw the young taipan's wife ahead of him. Having dropped his card in the box, he disregarded the legend "Out" and strode up to the door anticipating a welcome whisky and soda. He rang the bell. "I want to see Mrs Jameson." "Lady not at home." "But I saw lady go in." "Lady tellee me she not at home." "Then you tell lady that Hamish McTavish didna' call."

Perched high on Hong Kong's most fashionable eminence, taipans and their families felt themselves to be a world apart from those beneath them in status and location. Only after their servants walked out on them in response to a strike call in 1922 were Peakites reminded that they too could be subject to the stresses and strains of ordinary life.

4

SEAMEN'S STRIKE, 1922

"It will have done some good if it teaches us that we are living in a wholly different world from that which existed before the war. The strike has dispelled the illusion that we are immune from the dangers besetting the rest of the world."

South China Morning Post, *1922*

The first large-scale and successful labour strike in Hong Kong broke out in April 1920. Nine thousand mechanics working for twenty-six firms struck for higher pay, backed by the powerful Canton Mechanics' Union. The owners had to capitulate and the mechanics' terms were accepted.

In response, the government enacted an ordinance requiring all societies to register with the secretariat for Chinese affairs. The ninety-nine trade unions which had registered by 1921 indicated the growing strength of the labour movement in Hong Kong and caused the local correspondent of the *North China Herald* to comment: "The passing of an era brings us face to face with the fact that the good old days of guild relations with employees are disappearing, and more and more in the future we are likely to be faced with conflict between combinations of employees on the one hand and employers on the other."

The man responsible for steering Hong Kong through these more troubled waters was not really suited, by temperament or inclination, to the task. Sir Reginald Edward Stubbs, Hong Kong's governor from 1919 to 1925, was known at the Colonial Office as someone who used strong language and tended to get overexcited when dealing with the Chinese. He was highly suspicious of the new revolutionary movement sweeping south China and especially of its leader,

Sun Yat-sen. When, in opposition to warlord-dominated Peking, Sun was elected president of the Chinese Republic by Canton in 1921, Stubbs forebade the Chinese community in Hong Kong from holding any sort of celebration. The firing of crackers was forbidden, police squads patrolled the colony's main roads and back lanes and kept a strict watch over labour unions. Reflecting the views of its governor, the local English-language press labelled Sun's election "the Canton farce".

It was ironic that so much of the trouble in Hong Kong during these years was caused by the activities of Sun Yat-sen, who had in his youth been something of a golden boy in the colony. Sun was one of two students to gain the first licentiate in medicine when he graduated from the Hong Kong College of Medicine, the forerunner of the University of Hong Kong, in 1892. In its report of the exam results for that year, the *China Mail* revealed that Sun graduated with high distinction, having maintained a brilliant record throughout his five years as a student. In his final exams he headed the list in physiology, was equal first in anatomy, won the Watson scholarship, the Belilios botany prize, the Francis chemistry prize and was the prizeman in minor surgery and equal prizeman in clinical observations.

Coincidentally, on the very day that Sun first appeared in the Hong Kong press, the viceroy of Canton was expressing the hope that Hong Kong's College of Medicine would "through its students, be a blessing to China".

The kind of blessing Sun brought to China was not what the viceroy might have anticipated. Having qualified in Hong Kong to practise medicine, surgery and midwifery, Dr Sun went on to apply his brilliant mind to the dismemberment of the Manchu dynasty and the birth of the new Chinese Republic in 1911. He never lost sight of his debt to Hong Kong. In a speech to the Students' Union of Hong Kong University in February 1923 he declared that it was the extreme contrast between the backwardness and corruption of China and the peace, order and good government of Hong Kong which had first turned him into a revolutionary.

"Farcical" as events in Canton in 1921 may have seemed to the English, the influence of Sun's election posed serious threats to the status quo in Canton and Hong Kong. Following his inauguration, Sun introduced new labour laws which allowed the formation of trade unions. By the end of 1921 nearly every Canton union had gone on strike at least once and it was estimated that some sixty thousand Hong Kong workers, most of whom were native Cantonese, belonged to a union or guild in Canton or Hong Kong.

Hong Kong workers had every reason to take steps to improve their conditions. It was estimated that while the average monthly income of a Hong Kong worker in 1921 was twenty-five dollars, the required minimum for a man with a wife and one child to subsist on was at least thirty dollars a month. The situation had been made worse by a sharp rise in the cost of living after World War I. Food prices after 1919 shot up by forty per cent and the cost of polished rice, the staple Chinese diet, rose by a phenomenal 155 per cent. In addition, the value of the Hong Kong dollar fluctuated wildly, and the high cost of building, together with a growing demand for accommodation after the war, led to a sharp increase in rents. In July 1921 nearly eighty thousand workers belonging to more than a hundred labour unions signed a petition requesting the governor to curb exorbitant rent increases.

The frustrations of the coolie class in the face of these new pressures had already surfaced in the two-day rice riots of 1919. An angry crowd stormed rice shops in the main coolie area of Wanchai and looting spread to other poor areas of Hong Kong and Kowloon. The government responded by setting the price of rice at what it considered to be a reasonable maximum and punishing those arrested in the riots with heavy fines. A typical fine was fifty dollars imposed on a coolie employed at the cement works; as his earnings of ten dollars monthly made it impossible for him to pay the fine, he was obliged to do six weeks' hard labour instead.

The Hong Kong government, true to its policy of *laissez-faire*, was reluctant to deal positively with the basic problems facing the Hong Kong worker. When asked in the Legislative Council in the summer of 1921 whether the government would take steps to prevent compradores from raising the price of food and fuel, the colonial secretary, Claud Severn, replied that the government was "not disposed to interfere with retail trade in the colony" except in very urgent and exceptional circumstances.

The urgent and exceptional circumstances were not long in coming. Within six months of Severn's statement there occurred the first serious mass strike in Hong Kong, and it was led by the Chinese Seamen's Union. The rice riots of 1919 had only involved a section of the coolie class. The seamen's strike of 1922 was to make its impact felt throughout the length and breadth of the colony.

The Chinese Seamen's Union had originated as a secret organisation during the early years of the nationalist revolutionary movement in China when it assisted Sun Yat-sen in passing news from port to port. The union was formally set up in Hong Kong, with Sun's blessing, in February 1921. It was later assumed that Sun had instigated the strike to damage British interests and as revenge for the poor treatment he had received from the colony as a revolutionary in exile, but this was a claim he always strongly denied.

Whether or not Sun was behind the strike, the seamen themselves had very real grievances. In common with so many other workers in Hong

Kong, local seamen were at the mercy of the notorious contractor system. Shipping companies recruited their crews by using the services of a contractor who drew up a recruitment list of available seamen. To get on to the list the seamen had to pay an initial bribe of twenty dollars, or a month's wages, and subsequently up to sixty per cent of their earnings to stay on the list. The contractors did well enough on the proceeds to regularly pay as much as six thousand dollars' squeeze money to the agents of the shipping companies for the privilege of supplying a ship with labour.

Once on board a ship seamen worked fourteen hours a day and were often bullied by their better-paid European counterparts and by Chinese foremen; however, low pay and the contractor system were their basic grievances.

In September 1921 the seamen submitted their first petition to the shipping companies, requesting a wage increase from $20.00 to $29.50 a month. They also requested that the contractor system be abolished, suggesting instead that seamen be recruited through their union and that a union representative be present when contracts were signed. The petition, followed by a second, at first fell on deaf ears. The shipping companies were not even prepared to talk the matter over, and the government maintained a stony silence.

The government then had no specific department to deal with labour problems. The secretary for Chinese affairs was ostensibly responsible but could barely cope with all the other problems involving the Chinese in Hong Kong.

The seamen, meanwhile, were determined to have their grievances met. Twenty-three Chinese employers signed an undertaking to guarantee a wage increase, but the European shipping companies refused. In response, the union sent out a call to strike to all Chinese employed on ocean-going and river steamers calling at Hong Kong. The seamen had made arrangements with twelve other labour unions in Hong Kong to declare a sympathy strike, and on 29 January 1922 coolies all over Hong Kong walked out of their jobs to head back to their homes in China. They were joined by houseboys, cooks, office boys, printers, barbers, boiler-makers, electricians, tram conductors, fitters, tea-house waiters, Peak Tram drivers and even by mechanics whose pay and conditions were comparatively good. Perishable cargoes were left rotting on the wharves and in the holds of a hundred or more unmanned ships in the harbour.

The response of Sir Reginald Stubbs and the Hong Kong government was swift and fierce. Martial law was declared in the colony and armed military and naval posts were set up along the borders with China to stop the exodus of workers. The Seamen's Union was declared illegal because of its "attempts to paralyse the life of the colony by creating strikes among workmen who had no grievances against their employers". The union offices, together with the offices of the Tung Tak Guild and the Chap Yin Transportation Workers' Union, were raided and closed down. Union officials were arrested and the government began to commandeer labour. The police were authorised to search or seize any premises and arrest any persons they thought suspicious.

Armed military personnel assisted by American and British volunteers patrolled the waterfront and the Chinese business quarters where business had to be done behind closed doors, while Indian soldiers kept watch over the Kowloon suburbs.

The effects of the strike were keenly felt by those enjoying the privileges of Hong Kong expatriate life. Government House itself was left with only two Hakka staff, so the governor's retinue, and possibly even Sir Reginald himself, were forced to knuckle down to manual labour.

The Hong Kong Club announced that "the boys are out ... but arrangements have been made for tiffins on cafeteria lines". Café Wiseman, however, had to close down for the duration. Even J.H. Taggart, general manager of Hong Kong and Shanghai Hotels, rolled up his sleeves: he and his wife turned out 350 meals a day for the Hong Kong, Peak and Repulse Bay Hotels. Peggy Beard's parents were living in the Repulse Bay Hotel at the time, waiting for their new house in Lugard Road to be built. "All the servants disappeared and the residents had to work in the kitchens, a difficult thing to do when you're so accustomed to servants and don't know how to do anything."

Lane, Crawford and Dairy Farm kept going with the help of their European staff and volunteers. Dairy Farm's accountant, Mr Jack, more adept with pen and paper than with meat cleaver and chopping board, nearly severed his right hand while at work in the butchery department. With their cook boys on strike, housewives on the Peak had to learn to find their way around their own kitchens. There was a run on Mrs Beeton's cookery book in the colony's bookshops and the SS *Autolycus* sailed from London with a full assignment of Mrs Beetons to meet the growing demand. Without amahs, parents began to discover their children for the first time. Fathers learned to change nappies, and bridge parties were suspended in favour of playing with the children.

No European suffered physical violence at the hands of the Chinese, but the possibility was always there. A number of people connected with shipping received threatening letters, including Leung Yuk-tong, alias Jack Ah-tai, a senior partner in a firm of stevedores. On 24 February he was leaving the offices of Butterfield and Swire in a rickshaw when he was shot dead by a hired assassin. The fear that such incidents might escalate was never far from the surface. Events in the New Territories did not help matters.

Passenger traffic on the Kowloon-Canton railway had been closed down to prevent strikers leaving for Canton, where food was more readily available. On 4 March two thousand workers set off on a march to Canton, but were stopped by a police block at Shatin as they had no permits to leave Hong Kong. Troop reinforcements had failed to arrive because their bus had broken down, and assistant superintendent of police, Thomas Henry King, faced the mob with only a handful of policemen and soldiers to support him. King ordered the marchers to turn back and fired a warning shot. This had no effect, and the mob surged on. King gave orders to fire. Three of

the marchers fell dead and eight were wounded in what became known as the "Shatin Massacre". The reaction to the news of the killings was considerable and within three days the strike was over. Wage increases granted by the shipping companies came close to matching the seamen's demands and the government agreed to reinstate the Seamen's Union, together with the two other unions proscribed earlier. *The Hong Kong Daily Press* considered the settlement "deeply humiliating to the government and the foreign community".

The fifty-two day strike was the first real demonstration in Hong Kong of the strength of the Chinese worker. For many it was a chastening experience. According to the *South China Morning Post*, "It will have done some good if it teaches us that we are living in a wholly different world from that which existed before the war."

For the first time, Peak dwellers realised that without the Peak Tram or pack-horse coolies bringing supplies up to them, they were totally cut off and vulnerable. A new sympathy for the plight of the Chinese worker began to emerge among those living a more privileged life in Hong Kong, together with a sense of foreboding in the face of the power wielded by the coolie class when it was organised.

The Peak Residents' Association put forward the suggestion that returning houseboys should not be paid for the time they were out on strike, but instead resolved that this was a matter best left up to individuals. Most Peak residents, only too grateful to have their servants back, paid up willingly and some even gave their staff bonuses.

Many hoped that the colony had seen the end of such turmoil. But whether they liked it or not, events in Hong Kong could not be divorced from what was happening across the border, and the 1920s were tumultuous years for the Chinese Republic. As European and wealthy Chinese residents of Hong Kong settled back into their ordered, comfortable existence, little did they realise that within three years an even greater assault on the peace and prosperity of the colony would erupt, threatening its very existence.

5
GENERAL STRIKE, 1925

"To believe that the Chinese people are incapable of mass indignation and action and for acts of death and violence . . . is to imply that we are a people with the stuff of slaves in us . . . Great tidal waves of change have swept across the world, and men's work and action in this part of Asia are today inspired by ideas of freedom and human dignity which will not suffer them tamely to submit to violence and injustice."

A Chinese view of events in Hong Kong, 1925-26

"British power in the Orient has passed its peak."

Chiang Kai-shek, 1925

Britain's position in Hong Kong must be seen in the overall context of her involvement in China. From the 1840s onwards Britain was able to build herself up as the leading power in China due to a combination of superior naval power and the weakness of the ruling Manchu dynasty. By the end of the nineteenth century, however, her position was being challenged by Russia, Japan, Germany, France and the USA, and British policy became defensive rather than offensive. After 1902 she came to rely increasingly on an alliance with Japan to maintain her trade with China. To further safeguard her interests she was also forced to adopt a policy of conciliation towards the Chinese, remaining neutral during the 1911 Revolution even though she had hitherto been pro-Manchu and anti-revolutionary.

Throughout the warlord era which followed, Britain maintained a policy of supporting who-ever was in control in the capital, Peking, and it was this policy which caused her to misread events in the south which ultimately led to the great Hong Kong-Canton strike of 1925-26.

Commenting on British policy in the early 1920s, Sir Cecil Clementi, who as governor saw Hong Kong through the final stages of the strike, wrote in retrospect: "The British Foreign Office clung desperately to the illusion that Peking somehow or other governed all of China, even though it was clear that Peking had no control whatsoever in Kwangtung. Accordingly, when Sun Yat-sen, who was at that time dominant in Kwangtung, wished to be friends with Hong Kong and to get help from us, His Majesty's government decided that he must be treated as a rebel in arms against Peking and that British help could not be given to Canton."

Sun had repeatedly tried to get support from Britain and the USA from his base in Kwangtung province following his election there as president of China in 1921. He needed money to fight the warlords who still dominated much of China, including Peking, in order to unite the country under his rule and to introduce his concept of a just society based on socialist principles. Having failed to get support from Britain and America, it was logical that he should turn to Russia for help and in 1923 signed the Sun-Joffe agreement with the young bolshevik state. "Our faces are turned towards Russia, we no longer look to the Western powers."

Sun had good grounds for believing that Britain, through its position in Hong Kong, was trying to undermine his power in Kwangtung. On the other hand, Britain and the Hong Kong press felt justified in charging Sun with trying to "bolshevise" Canton, especially after the arrival of more than a hundred Russian agents, led by Mikhail Borodin, following the 1923 agreement. Britain and Hong Kong had every reason to be suspicious of Sun's intentions. Although not himself a communist, Sun had allowed the Chinese Communist Party to join his own Kuomintang Party as a means of strengthening his hand and winning over China's growing labour force.

By the end of 1925 the *Communist International* proudly proclaimed, "Canton is already very much like Moscow." Documents seized later during a raid on the Soviet military attaché's office in Peking showed that war supplies worth at least two and a half million roubles were forwarded to Canton in 1925-26. Hong Kong's Governor Stubbs reported that Russian steamers loaded with munitions and other military weapons regularly visited Canton, and it was also known that Russian money was being used to support the central bank of Canton.

Stubbs made no attempt to hide his hostility towards Sun Yat-sen and developments in Canton, an attitude which helped to intensify bad feeling between the two cities. Stubbs doubtless felt uneasy about the labour situation in Hong Kong, which he had done little to improve following the seamen's strike of 1922. He was also aware that the success of the 1922 strike had been largely due to Sun's old associate, Ch'en P'ing-sheng, and two communists, Lin Wei-min and the new president of the Seamen's Union, Su Chao-cheng.

However, it was the premature death of Sun Yat-sen in March 1925 and the bitter power struggle within his party in Canton which proved fatal to the interests of Hong Kong. The avowed aim of the left-wing Canton government which now emerged, advised as it was by the Russians,

was "to obtain the independence and freedom of China, the first step being the abolition of all unequal treaties", including those which had given Hong Kong, Kowloon and the New Territories to Britain.

The catalyst for an upsurge of anti-British feeling was provided by what the British euphemistically termed the "Shanghai Incident", which occurred on 30 May 1925 when British police at the international settlement fired on a mob of student demonstrators protesting foreign control in China, killing four outright and fatally wounding five. The so-called "massacre", as the Chinese media dubbed it, stimulated anti-foreign agitation throughout the country. Students and workers in Canton took to the streets, calling for a total boycott of British and Japanese trade.

Meanwhile, the Chinese Seamen's Union in Hong Kong, to commemorate the third anniversary of the 1922 strike, issued a manifesto addressed to the workers of the world. Five million copies were distributed in the colony and abroad denouncing Hong Kong and Sir Robert Ho-tung for allegedly plotting to defraud the seamen of their long-awaited strike pay. Lin Wei-min, a prominent member of the Seamen's Union, was voted in as chairman of the All-China Labour Federation, a communist organisation dedicated to overthrowing imperialism and capitalism.

On 17 June 1925 the secretary of the Seamen's Union, purporting to act on behalf of the union's Canton branch, instructed all Chinese seamen on foreign vessels in Hong Kong harbour to cease work immediately in protest "against the British imperialists who brutally massacred innocent Chinese at Shanghai". By the next day over a thousand Chinese seamen had left their jobs.

At the same time a propaganda campaign was begun to induce all Chinese people to leave Hong Kong. Posters were put up on lamp-posts along the waterfront and at tram stops informing the public that Hong Kong authorities intended to poison the colony's water and cut electricity supplies, that pitched battles would be fought in the streets and that the colony would be burned to the ground.

The seamen were immediately joined by Hong

Kong students, who showed their solidarity by staying away from school and adopting the slogan, "A foreign book in your hand makes you a subservient slave of the foreigners." Older students threatened to beat up younger ones if they did not join in, so fearful parents kept their children at home. On 18 June over half the students at the prestigious Queen's College were absent. Eighty per cent of the senior class missed their lessons in spite of the fact that important examinations were only days away. The summer vacation had to be put forward and, for the first time since the death of Queen Victoria, there was no speech day at Queen's College. Within a short time, all government schools had closed down, St Paul's and St Stephen's Girls being the last to do so.

By 19 June the Chinese staff at the Peak Hotel and the Peak Club walked out, followed by houseboys throughout the Peak district and staff from all the major hotels and restaurants in the colony. Stevedores and cargo coolies dropped their loads, drivers and conductors left their trams, messengers and office boys walked out of their offices. By 22 June market-stall holders had stopped work, as had the staff of the ferry companies and the Peak Tram. Government workers risked the loss of pension rights by dropping their pens and leaving secure employment in government offices, while nightsoil coolies washed their hands of their messy work, leaving buckets of human faeces unemptied.

By mid-July workers from most trades had left their jobs: journalists, compositors, delivery boys, laundrymen, ice-factory workers, telephone operators, pastry-makers, godown coolies, postmen, hospital coolies and tea-house cooks.

Hong Kong authorities considered the strike to be politically inspired, although Chinese workers undoubtedly had genuine industrial and social grievances. The Hong Kong Labour Commission, the body which had organised the strike locally, put forward a list of demands they wanted the government to meet. These included abolition of the contractor system and child labour, and the introduction of an eight-hour working day; the right of labour unions to vote for Chinese members of the Legislative Council; the right to be treated as the equals of Europeans; the abolition of the deportation law; an end to what they called "private torture and brutal assaults"; freedom of speech and of the press and the freedom to form guilds and hold public meetings; the reversal of the government's decision to allow landlords to increase rents by fifteen per cent, and a twenty-five per cent reduction in rents instead; and freedom for Chinese people to live on the Peak on the same basis as Europeans.

The call to strike was difficult to resist. Workers received threatening letters signed by the Blood and Iron Society and the Dare to Die Corps and imprinted with a dagger. After censorship of mail was imposed, scraps of paper were pushed through windows and under doors carrying the same message, "Join us or die." Telephone messages from anonymous callers promised death or torture to those who hesitated to join the strike. A week of such phone calls brought out the entire Chinese staff of *The Hong Kong Daily Press*. A few risked life and limb and the ignominy of their fellows by resisting such pressures. The chairman of the Chinese Engineers' Guild, Hon Man-wai, a chief mechanic at Hong Kong University, issued a bold manifesto to his men to keep gas and electricity supplies going. Rickshaw and sedan-chair coolies continued pulling, pushing and lifting Europeans around town: business was best for them in the hot summer and few could afford to give up their meagre earnings. Sampan people took advantage of the absence of launch crews to ferry travellers and their luggage to ocean liners at a dollar a head. A *Hongkong Telegraph* editorial praised rickshaw and chair coolies and sampan people as "the heroes of the strike".

The power of rumour was strong among the illiterate coolies, enabling strike agitators to spread false stories easily. Before long it was widely believed that the governor had been assassinated by an Indian soldier, that fifty thousand troops had invaded the New Territories from China and that all gas-holders were to be bombed. Chinese newspapers like the *San Man Po* churned out anti-British propaganda, branding

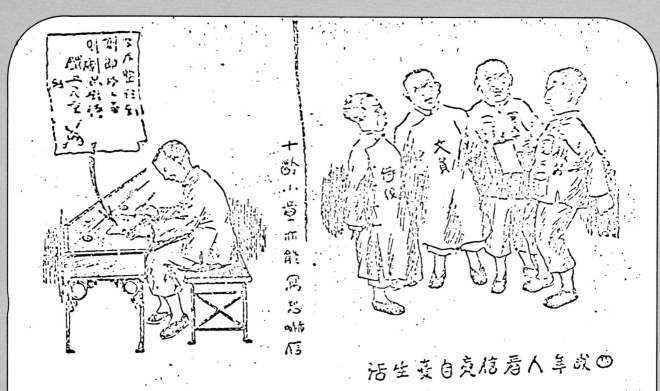

SOMETHING TO COUNTERACT STRIKE PROPAGANDA

The above represents a poster of which several thousands have been prepared to counteract the Cantonese agitators' efforts in Hongkong.

The man at the table is writing:—

"Friendly Labourers,—When this letter arrives you are to stop work immediately.

If you disobey we will deal with you forcibly.

"Signed by the Blood and Iron Child."

The characters down the middle say:—"Such letters can be written even by 10-year old children:"

The four men to the right are respectively labelled "Servant", "clerk", "tramwayman", "mechanic"; and the characters underneath say:—

"These four grown up persons after looking at these letters are willing to commit suicide so far as their livelihood is concerned."

North China Herald, *18 July, 1925.*

[HE CHINESE CRISIS.

STRIKE DECLARED IN HONGKONG.

TRAM SERVICE STOPS AND CHINESE PUBLIC SUFFERS.

AMPLE FOOD AND NO CAUSE FOR ALARM.

The Exodus to Canton.

THE SCHOOLS.

(To the Editor, S. C. M. Post.)

Sir.—As I am probably the only fool in the Colony who has not written to you about the strike, I must do so. I want to urge:

1. That schools start a little later in the morning. We find that it is hard to get children away in time.

2. That, should this trouble be going on when holidays are due, school should carry on a bit and relieve the parents of their children's presence.—Yours etc.,

COOLAMAH.

Hongkong, June 26, 1925.

South China Morning Post, *June 1925.*

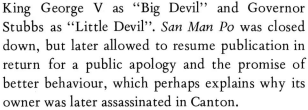

King George V as "Big Devil" and Governor Stubbs as "Little Devil". *San Man Po* was closed down, but later allowed to resume publication in return for a public apology and the promise of better behaviour, which perhaps explains why its owner was later assassinated in Canton.

An early tactic used by strike leaders was to distribute free train and boat tickets to Canton. A record number of twenty-five thousand passengers took the Kowloon-Canton railway to Shumchun in the first few weeks of the strike. The press of passengers to board steamers bound for Canton was so great that several people were killed in the crush to leave.

Once over the border strike pickets exerted pressure to prevent workers from returning to Hong Kong. Those caught trying to return were flogged in the streets of Canton or exposed for hours to the sun. Pearl River sampans going out to steamers bound for Hong Kong were seized and burnt. One woman was shot dead and three others drowned when they were caught trying to take fruit and vegetables from Shumchun into Hong Kong.

By early July Hong Kong was like a ghost town. Once again wives on the Peak had to learn how to cook and to look after their children. People used to a team of servants were accustomed to changing their clothes two or three times a day and wives now faced a daily pile of ironing. Men went to work in shorts which were easier to launder than the white duck suits they habitually wore.

A correspondent to the letters page of the *South China Morning Post* made the desperate suggestion that schools should remain open for the summer holidays to "relieve parents of their children's presence". The American community convened a special meeting at the US consulate and decided it would be inadvisable to hold their Independence Day celebrations that year.

The Sanitary Board issued emergency instructions for the disposal of nightsoil. People living on the Peak were to dispose of theirs by burying it in their gardens at a depth of no less than two feet; people on the lower levels could dump theirs in the sea, but not at Causeway Bay or the Harbour of Refuge. Sewer manholes marked with red paint were to be opened between 5.30 and 7.30 each morning at convenient points throughout the colony, although not on the Peak. Many in the lower levels stayed indoors for fear of asphyxiation, and the sale of gramophone records for home entertainment increased four-fold.

The Star Ferry, crewed by naval ratings, maintained a ten-minute service, with armed guards to protect the engine room. With ticket-sellers out on strike, only season-ticket holders were allowed on board. The Royal Navy ratings who manned the boats were unfamiliar with the machinery and controls and often found the cross-currents of the harbour harder to navigate than the high seas; there were inevitable delays and arrival at the Star Ferry pier was more often accomplished with a crash than a gentle bump. Public patience began to wear thin. A newspaper editorial of 28 June criticised the navy's "spotless uniforms and trailing impedimenta of silk handkerchiefs and lanyards", which were more suitable for Sunday church parade and the governor's guard of honour than for the tough business of working the cross-harbour ferries.

Missionaries and businessmen down from China also came in for a fair amount of criticism. "Those who idle away in the Hong Kong Hotel with nothing to do should be contributing voluntary service," said one correspondent. Most of the European anger, however, was inevitably directed at the Chinese. A *South China Morning Post* editorial summed up the general feeling: "We have submitted many times that half of the population of Hong Kong is entirely valueless. It comes here for the pickings. It produces nothing and does little work of any kind. It scarcely even consumes. It merely overcrowds the place."

Many Europeans left the colony. Steamship passages were fully booked; those without tickets offered to work as deck hands. The *Empress of Asia* sailed from Kowloon on at least one voyage with a crew of Hong Kong schoolmasters, Portuguese schoolboys and lady missionaries.

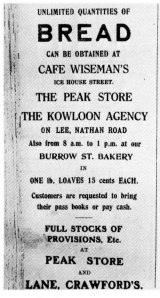

Among those who stayed the spirit of resistance and self-help was as strong as it had been in 1922. A strike concert at the Hong Kong Hotel attended by colony big-wigs raised money and morale. Accountants like Archie Ritchie of the firm of Lowe, Bingham and Matthews drove trams, lawyers lugged ice from Ice House Street, stockbrokers made the rounds collecting cables, bankers delivered parcels and letters to the Peak. An eminent local doctor carved joints in the kitchens of the Hong Kong Hotel. Elegant European ladies in white frilly aprons waited at table in the popular Café Wiseman, demanding cash rather than chit payment as the office staff were on strike. Café Wiseman supplied the colony with all its bread in the first week of the strike, announcing that though it could cope with bread supplies there would be no fancy loaves and cakes "except for children". Dairy Farm maintained stocks of frozen meat and organised the supply of food to the Peak. The Peak Club formed a special committee, led by Mrs Tratman, the wife of the secretary for Chinese affairs, to provide a baby-sitting service for wives doing their own shopping. Lane, Crawford took out a special advertisement in the *Hongkong Telegraph* giving a list of goods people should stock up with during the strike, but adding "come prepared to carry your purchases away".

Even the boys of disaffected Queen's College rallied to the cause and gave up their 1925 summer holiday to work for the survival of British Hong Kong. One boy drove a tram and a Portuguese contingent worked in the kitchens of the Repulse Bay Hotel. Teachers did duty at Dairy Farm in Wyndham Street and most of the loyal Chinese teaching staff worked on censorship for the government.

Governor Stubbs would not stand any nonsense. On 23 June he announced: "Those who disturb the peace of the colony will be treated, as is the way with the English, justly but sternly. Any attempts at disorder will be relentlessly suppressed."

A state of emergency was declared in the colony. Stubbs invoked emergency powers to censor the mail, the vernacular press and all cables. The police were given the right to search and seize suspicious persons and undertook raids on areas of the colony like Jardine's Bazaar and Hollywood Road, where seditious literature, printing presses and firearms were most likely to be kept.

Food, transport and labour controls were established, special police were enrolled and the Hong Kong Volunteers were called up. A military show of force was organised, with naval and military units and the Volunteers marching through the western and eastern coolie districts. Leslie Ralph remembers being given time off work to do patrols, but lamented having to leave the office at the most inconvenient times. For him, strike duty had its compensations, though: "It was really a glorified pub crawl as we went from club to club." For Harry Owen Hughes, night patrols in Wanchai were rather more hazardous: "Things were thrown at us from third-floor windows." Nevertheless, he maintained a confidence which was in keeping with the spirit of the British empire: "There was a bit of unpleasantness which the people of England knew how to tackle." However, the survival of Hong Kong was also due to the efforts of other nationalities and races. Many Chinese joined the Volunteers and Special Police Reserve and over a hundred signed up for the St John's ambulance brigade. The latter risked their lives by wearing the same uniform as the Volunteers; when the government was asked if St John's workers could wear distinctive armbands, permission was refused on the grounds that the more Chinese who were mistaken for Volunteers the better and the sight of Red Cross armbands might create panic over the fear of invasion.

To counter adverse propaganda and the spread of rumour, the government decided to produce its own propaganda. Responsibility for this was given to two pillars of the Chinese community, Chow Shou-son and Robert Kotewall, both unofficial members of the Legislative Council. On behalf of the government they published their own newspaper, the *Kung Sheung Yat Po*, which later became a permanent newspaper in private hands. At that time it was used for counter-propaganda and stressed the bolshevik nature of the strike. A major problem they had to face was getting the paper printed.

The only regular Chinese newspaper to keep going throughout the strike was the *Wah Kiu Yat Po*, but when Kotewall and Chow approached its owners and various printing firms to have the *Kung Sheung Yat Po* printed the workers mysteriously disappeared. Only the Victoria gaol press could be relied upon, and even then not

entirely: more than one prisoner (accidentally?) dropped the typeset frame, scattering letters all over the floor.

Nevertheless, the government paper was in print by the second week of July and copies were sent to leading overseas Chinese communities in America and Australia who had hitherto been financing the strikers in Canton. Such counter-propaganda, together with telegrams sent by the Tung Wah Committee warning overseas Chinese against the "Red terror" in Canton, were enough to convince America's most powerful overseas Chinese association, the Chi Kung Tong, to pass resolutions condemning the Canton Reds.

To win over the illiterate population Kotewall and Chou employed street orators at sixty dollars a month to harangue coolies against joining the strike. Mr Kong Kit-tong was stoned twice when he addressed crowds at the Chinese recreation ground, but was later given a bodyguard by the Labour Protection Bureau, which had been set up by a retired Chinese general, Leung Wing-sun. The bureau, with its headquarters in a requisitioned boarding house, was never openly mentioned in the press but everyone knew of its existence. Leung employed 150 henchmen, most of them thugs and ex-pirates, to protect workers who stayed at their jobs. Their strong-arm methods aroused adverse criticism. The government, however, took the line that it had to find bold men to "intimidate the intimidators" and that, as boldness was a rare quality among the Chinese, it could only be found in those with somewhat adventurous backgrounds. Kotewall was a little more explicit: "Though it is necessary that our agents for this dangerous work should act for us in a clean way, they should not be required to furnish proof of having worn kid gloves from their youth up."

Stubbs turned a blind eye to the activities of the Labour Protection Bureau but took a firm line with those caught as "intimidators". As punishment they were put to work removing nightsoil and rubbish from the streets. Stubbs explained, with a certain amount of glee, that by giving them such "useful, though somewhat

Volunteers in white summer kit, 1920.

Stockbroker Alec Hutton Potts (centre) was commander of the Mounted Machine Gun Troop.

Volunteer headquarters, 1920. The headquarters were on the site of the present west wing of the government offices in Garden Road.

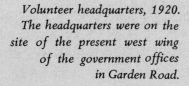

M. G. Troop.—H.K.V.D.C.
"Dowbiggin's Trophy" Dinner.
Hunter's Arms.—April 9th, 1932.

*"Dowbiggin's Boys", 1932.
The Mounted Machine Gun
Troop of the Volunteers
in formal and informal pose.*

*Governor Sir William Peel
and officers of the Hong Kong
Volunteers Defence Corps
at camp in the New Territories,
early thirties.*

unattractive duties" he was offering them the chance of "proving their value to humanity". A more drastic remedy was flogging. "They will in future be dealt with in a manner which will be likely to appeal to their deepest feelings — that is, by 'the cat'!"

The Hong Kong community heartily approved. In Canton, however, the proposal to introduce flogging was seen as yet another example of British imperialistic brutality, while in London the Foreign Office was susceptible to Chinese feelings and to those expressed in a *Manchester Guardian* leader article, "... fighting speeches may be excellent at English elections; they are less excellent in the mouth of a British governor explaining the attitude of his government towards a large body of the nationals of a power with whom our formal relations are still friendly, though critical."

British public opinion was essentially unsympathetic to the plight of their fellow countrymen in Hong Kong. The universal impression "back home" was that the whole trouble was fundamentally industrial and that the strike represented a just revolt of workers against conditions long since abolished in Britain.

Accordingly, Stubbs was forced to back down, having been warned by the secretary of state for the colonies, Leo Amery, that if flogging were introduced there might well be retaliation against British nationals in China and fierce opposition from the USA. Indeed, American public opinion, already incensed by reports of the Shanghai massacre, was further inflamed against British imperialism when the news of a second "massacre" came a month later. Foreign personnel in Canton had fired on an angry crowd of demonstrators advancing on the British concession at Shameen, killing fifty and wounding over a hundred. The "Shameen Massacre" of 23 June played right into the hands of the Chinese authorities, who interpreted it as a classic case of British aggression against unoffending Chinese

workers. Drawing a parallel to the massacre at Amritsar in 1919, which had done so much to weaken Britain's position in India, the Chinese caustically referred to Shameen as "action based on the doctrines of preventive massacre which specialists of drastic action are wont to advise as a magic operation with Oriental crowds".

Anglo-American, as well as Hong Kong-American, relations were placed under further strain by a set of resolutions put out by the American staff of the Canton Christian College (also known as Lingnan College) following events at Shameen. The seventeen American missionary staff expressed their "horror and regret" at the "merciless and unjustified" shooting and assured the Chinese they would use their influence with the US government to persuade it to help China free herself from imperialism.

Although the statement was later retracted by the college president, the damage was already done, at least as far as Hong Kong was concerned. Americans in the colony had to lie low until the hullabaloo died down, and when one of the original signatories to the petition, a Mr Graybill, arrived in Hong Kong in mid-July, he was informed by the authorities that it would be advisable if he voluntarily left the colony as soon as possible.

The Shameen incident did much to strengthen the resolve of Chinese workers to continue their fight against Hong Kong. It also resulted in the decision of the Hong Kong-Canton Strike Committee, the powerful body widely regarded as "the second government of Canton", to supplement the strike by a full-scale economic boycott of Hong Kong. "Hong Kong is the throat of China's economy, she has a stranglehold over us. Let us throttle her and open up a new outlet of our own at Canton."

Canton's resolve to throttle Hong Kong through a trade boycott in the course of the next year was to prove a much greater danger to the colony's existence than the strike alone had been.

6

BOYCOTT

"Hong Kong is the leading trading port of south China and commands the economy of the whole area. If the stranglehold on her trade continues, one can only envisage a pessimistic future for Hong Kong and south China."

Wah Tze Yat Po, *25 November 1925*

Following the Hong Kong-Canton Strike Committee's announcement of a trade boycott against Hong Kong on 6 July 1925, pickets began searching all incoming ships at Canton for British goods or goods imported from Hong Kong and prevented all British ships and ships from Hong Kong from entering any Kwangtung port.

The boycott was largely a response to an earlier attempt by Stubbs to impose a blockade on Canton. Stubbs had hoped to break Canton as a means of ending the strike in Hong Kong, but soon found that the only way of stopping foodstuffs and other goods entering Canton was by establishing a full naval blockade. With only a small fleet of ships at his disposal this proved to be impossible.

The Canton boycott of Hong Kong was an entirely different matter. The only way Hong Kong merchants could trade with Canton was to ship their goods eight hundred miles to Shanghai and then south to Canton by train. Even so, they had to erase all marks identifying their goods with Britain or Hong Kong. It was a costly, time-consuming and frustrating business, with little financial return. As the effects of the boycott began to bite, Hong Kong's trade became paralysed. Statistics are hard to come by, as Stubbs abolished the statistical office of the Imports and Exports Department, but it is known that in the course of 1925 and 1926 less than half

the number of vessels cleared the Harbour Office as compared to 1924. Hong Kong's life-blood in those days was the entrepôt trade with south China and the flow of its three most important commodities was virtually at a standstill. The transhipment of textiles, rice and silk was, in the words of a prominent local dealer, "literally dead".

Food prices in the colony rose six-fold and it is estimated that the boycott cost Hong Kong between three hundred and five hundred million dollars in gold. There had earlier been a run on Chinese banks following the outbreak of the strike in June 1925, with millions of dollars being transferred out of the colony or hoarded away. At that time the Chinese banks had to close for a week and only reopened after being given a six million dollar loan by the Hongkong and Shanghai and the Chartered Banks. As the full effects of the boycott began to be felt, there was a second run on Chinese banks in September 1925. At the same time a deputation of businessmen and bankers approached Stubbs for a £3,000,000 trade loan from Britain. Stubbs passed on the request to the Colonial Office, but with anti-British feeling at its height in China the British government was loath to assist Hong Kong "for reasons of world politics".

The Colonial Office itself had long experienced difficulty in getting money out of the British treasury, leading one Colonial Office man to complain bitterly that the treasury was in the habit of "taking all the money they can get from the Far Eastern colonies, including generous gifts, and refusing to give them any assistance whatever, in their hour of need".

That Hong Kong's hour of need had come was clear to all who lived in the colony. The share market, which reopened in October following its collapse in June, suffered an overall depreciation of forty per cent in the value of stocks and shares traded. Many businesses declared insolvency. By September the bankruptcy court was dealing with twenty cases a day. Land values tumbled and the consequent collapse in government land sales, together with a decline in harbour revenue, deprived the government of one million dollars in income by the end of 1925.

Meanwhile, in London, the Colonial Office was finally able to promise Stubbs the loan he had requested. The funds were to come from the West African Currency Board and from the Straits Settlements. Stubbs immediately had the good news published in all the newspapers.

However, for Stubbs, such financial help was only a stop-gap measure, which eased the colony's financial problems but did nothing to end the boycott. What he was really after was British military support to destroy the Canton government and end the boycott by force. In telegrams to London he urged Britain to impose a naval blockade in the Pearl River, bomb the Bocca Tigris forts and give massive financial support to Chinese warlords who were prepared to march south against the bolshevists in Kwangtung.

Britain, however, adamantly refused to take any action which might stir up further anti-British sentiment in China. The Colonial Office became very impatient with Stubbs and his blunt demands. "Sir R.E. Stubbs is in the habit of using such strong language that he leaves no margin for impressing on us and the Foreign Office the gravity of such a situation as in the present."

Unlike Stubbs, the Colonial Office did not have to deal directly with an angry Hong Kong public. There was a very strong feeling in Hong Kong that not enough was being done to end the boycott.

Mr P.H. Holyoak, chairman of the Hong Kong General Chamber of Commerce and an unofficial member of the Legislative Council, voiced the general attitude of the British in Hong Kong that they were being abandoned by their government at home, when he spoke at a mass meeting of British expatriates in August: "Does His Majesty's government still utterly disbelieve responsible statements made in the stream of cables of the gravest nature by the governor of this colony and all the responsible bodies already on the spot . . . , or do they seriously profess that they are unable any longer to protect, or at any rate are prepared to abandon the rights of the British subjects secured to them by foreign treaty, and will they supinely submit to the latest insolent challenges to Great Britain of the present Cantonese bolshevist regime?"

The feelings of the British in Hong Kong were even more fiercely expressed against the house-boys who had deserted them. Gone was the indulgent attitude of 1922. At a separate mass meeting at the Peak Club on 25 July 1925, the British community decided to withhold wages from their servants for the time they were on strike should the "ingrates" return.

The London Telegraph, however, reflected English public opinion when it commented: "Does it not seem rather uncomplimentary to . . . the Hong Kong government . . . that the community should continue to hold mass meetings at which a certain amount of hot air and possibly tactless utterances will be released?"

Chinese businessmen in Hong Kong could not be as vocal in their demands as their British counterparts, because they had family and long-standing business ties with Kwangtung, which they did not wish to sever. Nevertheless, they privately supported British merchants in their efforts to end the boycott. In the absence of official British support against Canton they took the initiative in raising money, with Stubbs' approval, for a warlord army to march on Canton. On 25 August a Cantonese general, Wei Bong-ping, arrived in Hong Kong to ask for one million dollars to finance an expedition against Canton. He was interviewed by Chow Shou-son, Robert

Kotewall, the colonial secretary and the secretary for Chinese affairs, who jointly agreed to raise the money. Chinese merchants found it difficult to come up with the cash, so the Tung Wah Hospital Committee was approached. Reluctantly, the committee agreed to foot the bill.

Wei Bong-ping's attempted *coup d'état* in Canton failed miserably, and all but one of the syndicate of merchants were unable to repay Tung Wah. The new governor, Sir Cecil Clementi, saved the situation by paying Tung Wah back from the trade loan secured by Stubbs. The Colonial Office took a dim view of the money it had raised with such difficulty to rescue Hong Kong's economy being used to finance an obscure warlord in an abortive attempt to overthrow Canton.

Sir Cecil Clementi was a very different man from his predecessor. Whereas Stubbs was brusque and called a spade a spade, Clementi understood the subtleties of Chinese culture and politics and had a deep sympathy for the Chinese people. Unlike Stubbs, he spoke Cantonese and Mandarin and was a respected Chinese scholar. However, Clementi's appointment in 1925 initially aroused the suspicions of the British community in Hong Kong, who regarded him as being "pro-Chinese".

Nevertheless, Clementi knew that to end the boycott it was necessary to improve relations with Canton and, from the start, worked hard on rebuilding the bridges which Stubbs had allowed to fall into such disrepair. Negotiations with Canton had never been a part of Stubbs' vocabulary, but Clementi realised that the boycott could only be ended once Hong Kong — and Britain — afforded recognition to those in power in Kwangtung. "The sooner the present sore which is festering and may become chronic can be healed, the better it will be for British interests not only in Hong Kong, but throughout China," he told the Foreign Office.

The task of forging links with Canton was an awesome one. At first, Hong Kong's governor had little if any contact even with Britain's official representative in Canton, as they were separately responsible to the Colonial Office and the Foreign Office respectively. Stubbs had not been on speaking terms with Britain's consul-general in Canton, James William Jamieson, and Jamieson himself had very little contact with the Canton government, who regarded him as "most difficult". Jamieson had spent much of his time in Canton behind "his absurd wires and sandbags piled up on the bund" for fear of assassination should he venture beyond the British concession at Shameen.

By the time Clementi took over as governor, Hong Kong's Chinese merchants had suffered the boycott for nearly half a year. They were now prepared to pay off the strikers to end the strike and boycott. To an Englishman of Clementi's high principles, the idea of resorting to what he considered blackmail was repugnant. Nevertheless, it seemed to be the only way out and was in any case preferable to the alternative of outright war against Canton. "The time is passed when it is possible for foreign nations at the point of the bayonet to compel the Chinese to trade with them."

Clementi understood the significance of "face" in Chinese life. He also knew that for the strikers and the Canton government to end the boycott and renege their avowed aim of ending imperialism would involve a serious loss of face. One way to avoid this was to take the matter to the League of Nations, but this idea was quashed by the British government, who took the view that it would be a pointless measure because the other interested party, the USA, was not a member of the League. Britain was also wary of giving China the opportunity to air her anti-British grievances on the world stage in Geneva. Another possibility which was given short shrift was for Britain to apply pressure on Moscow to end Borodin's anti-British activities in Canton. The Kremlin consistently denied that it had anything to do with the troubles in south China, as Borodin worked for the *Third Communist International* and not the Russian government. In any case, Britain had very little political leverage when it came to dealing with the Soviets.

Clementi felt that the best solution was for Britain to abandon the fiction that the Peking government had authority over the whole of China and to offer recognition to the Canton government as a precondition for ending the boycott. He also hoped that Britain would help Canton build a loopline connecting the Kowloon-Canton railway with the Canton-Hankow railway and so promote China trade in the interests of both Hong Kong and Canton.

Britain, however, was determined to maintain a policy of inaction. Its whole China policy was set by the Washington Treaty of 1922, which laid down that no action could be taken in China without the approval of the other signatory powers. Britain took the attitude that events in China would eventually sort themselves out. "Our policy in China has been to regard that country as in a state of transition and of abnormal conditions, to which ordinary rules do not apply. We believe that patience and non-interference are the only means by which a satisfactory solution can be reached."

As it turned out, Britain proved to be right. Events in Canton took an unexpected turn, which led to the Cantonese calling off the boycott. On 20 March a *coup d'état* in the city resulted in the emergence of Chiang Kai-shek as the new strongman and a decline in the influence of left-wing radicals. Chiang was primarily concerned with launching his Northern Expedition against the warlords as a final step in uniting China under Kuomintang rule. The last thing he wanted was to have to deal with the troubles in Hong Kong. Furthermore, he hoped to obtain a loan from Hong Kong to help finance the costly expedition north.

It was under these circumstances that the Kuomintang government in Canton officially ended the boycott on 10 October 1926. As the civil war in China moved northwards during the course of 1927, relations between Canton and Hong Kong steadily improved. *Entente* between the two cities was symbolised by an interchange of visits between Clementi and the new head of the Canton government, Marshall Li Chai-sum, to their respective cities, and a visit to Canton by the British minister Sir Miles Lampson. Hong Kong, moreover, benefited in the years ahead from

This cleverly-conceived cartoon, by Mr. J. Alvares, depicts the Malayan Tiger bearing away Sir Cecil Clementi from the Colony in which he has spent the greater part of his official career.

Sir Cecil Clementi had won the admiration of all communities for his part in helping to end the strike and boycott. A brilliant governor, all the major developments of the next decade were largely the result of his initiatives. He went on to become governor of the Straits Settlements and high commissioner of the Federated Malay States.

Britain's conciliatory policy towards China. Before long, Britain had handed over to Chiang Kai-shek the British concessions in Hankow and Weihaiwei.

Clementi had realised his ambition of forging links with the Chinese and, in the subsequent years of his governorship, he did all he could to promote better relations between Europeans and Chinese in Hong Kong. The two communities were brought together at social gatherings held at Government House. While Stubbs had always been strongly against appointing Chinese officials to the highest levels of the colonial government, believing that "the general indifference of the Chinese to all matters of public life was almost unbelievable", Clementi took the revolutionary step in May 1926 of appointing the first Chinese to the Executive Council. Clementi was frequently critical of the racial exclusiveness of many of Hong Kong's clubs and even suggested replacing the Hong Kong Club with one in which both British and Chinese members would be welcome.

In this Clementi was way ahead of his time. But his initiatives, together with the traumatic effects of the general strike and boycott were, in the long run, to create a greater sense of communion between the two races in Britain's tiny outpost of empire.

THE HONG KONG HOTEL FIRE

The fire in Hong Kong's most prestigious hotel started at eight o'clock in the morning on New Year's Day, 1926. It began with a fusing of wires in a lift shaft and caught hold on the fifth floor. The whole building may well have been engulfed had the wind been up and the residents not been available, thanks to the night before, to help hotel staff contain the blaze in its early stages. Hoses were quickly laid, but the pressure of water was insufficient to reach the upper floors, so the fire brigade was brought in, supported by detachments (including Prince George) from all warships in the harbour, the dockyard fire brigade, police and men from the East Surrey regiment. Within an hour flames licking up Des Voeux Road and Pedder Street could be clearly seen from Kowloon. The whole colony was soon in attendance. Pumps were kept going throughout Saturday and Sunday while arc lamps transformed night into day. Furniture, beds, bags and baggage were strewn along Pedder Street and Des Voeux Road, splintered, broken, sodden and totally irreparable.

Business at the hotel continued as usual in spite of the raging inferno in one wing. Fifty-cent afternoon teas were transferred from the burnt-out lounge to the cafeteria;

Fighting the flames from Des Voeux Road.

The front entrance of the Hong Kong Hotel from Pedder Street

48

Bessie's Bar and the dining room did business as usual. Tea dances on the Roof Garden were temporarily suspended as it was thought that dancing on the roof of a burning building was rather too optimistic a venture, but the band was ready to perform for tea dances by the following Monday.

Fire damage was estimated at two and a half million dollars, but luckily the fire had affected only one part of the hotel. There was one fatality: Able Seaman E.E. Batchelor, a twenty-eight year old Londoner, had been standing on a first-floor ledge trying to break some locked shutters, despite warnings not to do so, when he slipped and fell into an alleyway below. He was rushed to hospital with arms and legs broken, and died later. Some may have regarded his action as foolhardy and his death as avoidable, but he was nevertheless accorded a full naval funeral and wreaths were laid "to one of Britain's heroes". Able Seamen Batchelor was certainly a fighter: he had only been released from hospital the day before for injuries received in the boxing ring.

The burnt-out wing.

7

ENTERTAINMENT

"A writer of many excellent works, Ravel's name came much before the Hong Kong public recently because of the popularity of 'Bolero' following its incorporation into a film starring George Raft."

Obituary notice on the French composer Ravel,
South China Morning Post, *1938*

"Hong Kong is a lovely place, but what a pity there is so little to do."

Tourist's comment, *1935*

Like those who dressed formally for dinner in tents deep in the African bush, the European in Hong Kong adhered to an unofficial but strict form of protocol. Breakfast, tiffin, high tea and dinner were served by a houseboy in good English china, with sterling silver accessories carefully arranged on a crisp, white tablecloth.

Dinner, even without guests, was an especially formal affair. According to Marjorie August, who always changed into a long dress for the evening meal, "You never thought of sitting down for dinner in the same clothes you'd worn all day. There was soup, fish, meat and sweet and savoury desserts, all served on to the plate by the Number One boy. This was just for ordinary meals. If you had people in for dinner there would be seven courses, with cocktails beforehand and coffee and liqueurs to finish."

Bridge was a must for those wanting a full social life. Eric Himsworth was never much of a bridge player, but he remembers the formality of bridge parties. "You always dressed for dinner, in black tie and dinner jacket. You would arrive at a quarter to eight — the time never seemed to vary — just enough time for two gins. At eight o'clock you moved into the dining room and ate until a quarter past nine, after which you

adjourned to the drawing room for the game of bridge, which finished at eleven o'clock."

Peggy Beard's mother was a fairly unusual Peak woman in that she didn't play bridge at all. Her advice to her daughter was, "Don't you ever start playing bridge, you'll be at it all day." When not out shooting at the Ladies' Recreation Club, she might be at home doing needlework or entertaining friends at tea parties with a full spread, laid on by the houseboy, of scones, tea cakes and cucumber sandwiches.

There was a good deal of home entertainment — people were invited over for mah-jong, sing-songs accompanied by piano, accordion or Hawaiian guitar, or evenings of charades and parlour games purchased from Lane, Crawford. Ships in the harbour provided a good alternative to home as a venue for parties. The Raven sisters were often escorted by officers to parties on board the floating HMS *Tamar*, the Butterfield and Swire coastal boats or the great P & O and Blue Funnel ocean liners. One year they saw in the New Year aboard a walla-walla, which had broken down in the middle of the harbour on its way to a party on the *Empress of Asia*.

Quiet evenings at home might be spent practising pieces on the piano or accordion, winding up the gramophone, writing letters, playing solitaire, catching up on news from a wide choice of English-language newspapers or, after the first wireless broadcasting studio was set up at the post office in 1929, listening to ZBW programmes on the colony's early receiving sets.

The quality of broadcasting in the early days was variable, as technical facilities at the small ZBW station in Central were fairly primitive. In 1930 one man on duty served as electrical engineer, programme arranger, talent selector, announcer, studio artiste and secretary. With the growing popularity of gramophone records, public tolerance of live broadcasts from the ZBW studios wore increasingly thin. "I enjoy a good lecture, be it serious or light; a studio play, or a verbal or instrumental solo which we cannot get locally in record form," declared a 1930 listener, "but why have we got to listen to local talent singing and playing numbers which the greatest artistes of the world have given us on record?" Amina el Arculli was one example of local talent, performing her first ZBW broadcast at the age of sixteen with Brahm's 'Sandman' and a musical rendering of 'Where the bee sucks there suck I'. She had a beautiful voice, trained by the virtuoso Gualdi, Hong Kong's foremost singing teacher, but she could hardly compete with the best gramophone recordings. ZBW's philosophy was based on the Protestant ethic of the BBC's founding father, Sir John Reith, who held that it was not the calling of the new medium to give the public what it wanted, but to provide "education, information and entertainment" – in that order. As there was only one station, the Hong Kong public could exercise no choice in listening once they had bought a receiving set. Sales of wirelesses were very slow in the early days and, with little money coming in from the purchase of licences, the ZBW producers had little to work with.

Even in the late thirties dance music was forbidden on Sundays. Listeners to ZBW on the Sabbath heard only classical and military music, interspersed with news and talks aimed at improving mind and soul. Many Hong Kong listeners reacted against such a heavy diet. "Through a printer's error yesterday's ZBW programme contained Haydn's Concrete in D Major," complained one listener, adding, "as if the stuff was not heavy enough."

A show at the pictures provided a popular evening out, with the latest films from Hollywood and a newsreel. The newsreels were made for entertainment rather than information, with clips about donkey derbies, "Rigorous Rugger" at Twickenham, "Wedlock at Much Wenlock" and "Highlights of Hamburg" interspersed with news of the rise of the Nazis, the general election and Britain's military capabilities, all delivered by the newsreader in a uniformly lighthearted way.

The King's was the first cinema to introduce air-conditioning in the late thirties, followed by the Queen's. In its early days the new invention, pioneered in the colony by the Hongkong and Shanghai Bank, was, according to Marjorie Angus, "so cold that lots of people went down with pneumonia".

An evening out at the pictures was a formal affair in the twenties. Dress Circle meant exactly that. "You weren't allowed into the pictures unless you wore evening dress. Unless, of course, you sat in the stalls, which no European I knew ever did as the Chinese sat there," recalls Marjorie Angus. One of her favourite cinemas was the Star, at the corner of Ashley and Hankow Roads in Kowloon. "You didn't sit in individual seats, but on couches with white covers on them. They sagged in the middle so when you sat in them you were thrown against your partner. It was very nice, too." The World cinema also had couches and, for Chinese audiences in the stalls, the added attraction of a Chinese translator. Marjorie Angus remembers him sitting in "a sort of throne on one side of the stage. He read out the subtitles in Cantonese. It was very annoying as you couldn't hear what the actors were saying."

By the late thirties there were seven cinemas showing the latest Hollywood movies. The choice of films was good. Taking a random week, 1-8 January 1938, you could see Astaire and Rogers in Gershwin's *Shall we Dance?* at the Central,

King's theatre,
1938.

ZBW Programming for New Year's Day, 1938.

12.00–12.30 p.m.	Relay of a special service from St John's Cathedral.
12.30–1.00 p.m.	Peter Dawson (bass baritone) singing with the BBC radio orchestra.
1.00 p.m.	Time signal and weather report.
1.03–1.30 p.m.	A dance tune medley by the New Mayfair Orchestra including, 'Sweet Adeline', 'When You're Only Seventeen' and 'Sorrento by the Sea'.
1.30 p.m.	The Reuter press report, followed by the weather and announcements.
1.40–1.56 p.m.	Selections from Gilbert and Sullivan.
1.56–2.15 p.m.	Variety show featuring Max Miller comedy and Coleman Hawkins on saxophone.
2.15–2.30 p.m.	Dance music with the Harry Roy Orchestra.
2.30–6.00 p.m.	Station close down.
6.00–7.00 p.m.	A programme in Chinese.
7.00–8.00 p.m.	Grand variety programme, featuring the Leicestershire Brass Band, Paul Robeson, piano selections, and drinking songs played by the Jack Hylton Orchestra.
8.00 p.m.	Time signal, weather and announcements.
8.03–8.50 p.m.	Cello music.
8.50–9.00 p.m.	"London Log", a talk by E.A. Montague.
9.00–9.30 p.m.	Compositions by Grieg.
9.30–9.50 p.m.	The news from London.
9.50–Midnight	Relay of the dance orchestra from the Hong Kong Hotel, interspersed with five-minute intervals of recorded music from ZBW. Tunes include 'Penthouse on Third Avenue', 'Love Is Never Out of Season', 'Night over Shanghai', 'Blue Hawaii', 'Seranade in the Night', 'You Can't Run Away from Love' and 'Swing is here to stay'.

Queen's theatre,
1938.

AT LAST! A BIG STAGE SHOW AGAIN!
The Outstanding Musical and Theatrical Attraction of Recent Years.

THEATRE ROYAL

Short Season Commencing *Monday January 26*

Important:—

BOX PLANS FOR THE SEASON WILL OPEN AT MOUTHIE'S NEXT MONDAY, JAN. 19th. Reserves only $4.

Edward Branscombe has the Honour to Present, on Their 4th Tour of the World, his Sixteen Renowned.

WESTMINSTER GLEE SINGERS

In their Unique and Fascinating Entertainments, of the Folk Songs of England, Ireland, Scotland and Wales, Glees, Character Comedy Scenas, Anthems, and Hilarious Sailors' Shanteys, with the GLORIOUS SINGING OF 10 FRONT RANK MALE SOLOISTS and 6 DELIGHTFUL BOY SOPRANOS.

The Bowen Players, 1930. In the New Year's Eve concert at the Bowen Road military hospital in 1930 the staff put on a comedy revue.

Laurel and Hardy in *Way Out West* at the King's, Marlene Dietrich in *Angel* at the Queen's, Spencer Tracey and Lionel Barrymore in Kipling's *Captain Courageous* at the Majestic on Nathan Road, *Merry-Go-Round of 1938* at the Alhambra, Bing Crosby in *Double or Nothing* at the Oriental in Wanchai and Benjamino Gigli in *Forget Me Not* at the Star in Hankow Road, Kowloon.

The tradition of amateur dramatics was also strong in Hong Kong, as it was throughout the empire. The City Hall had provided the 'Theatre Royal' as a venue for Amateur Dramatic Society productions. Opened in the City Hall in 1869, there were few tears shed when the delapidated old building was demolished in the thirties. A 1932 editorial in the *South China Morning Post* admitted that the theatre and public rooms of the City Hall had fallen into disuse due to the "uninviting interior of the block" and because new cinemas put on shows by travelling companies and music stars.

However, there was no other suitable public building. "Where are new governors to be publicly welcomed on arrival, or distinguished visitors received? . . . What we need is a thoroughly up to date assembly hall, with smaller rooms suitable for chamber music and dramatics, a real public library, a worthwhile museum and maybe an art gallery," was one suggestion put forward in the early thirties.

The old City Hall had also housed Hong Kong's only museum, which had, by the thirties, become a resting place for coolies seeking shelter and a snooze. The specimens it housed, apart from the dozing coolies, included stuffed Australian parrots, mineralogical specimens from Wales, old clocks and un-named sea shells. By 1937, the specimens had been attacked by insects, dry rot, neglect and typhoons. It was therefore not surprising that a 1937 survey carried out by the Carnegie Corporation of New York came to the conclusion that Hong Kong represented the "low water mark in museum provision for the whole of the empire, with the exception of the smaller islands of the Pacific and the more backward African territories".

Circuses and travelling shows periodically arrived by steamship and played to packed houses for a few weeks. In 1938, a Russian circus performed in Kowloon, while the Marcus Show of 1939 titillated audiences with its daring displays of female flesh. The *Overland China Mail* reported: "Twenty minutes after the *President Cleveland* had docked, the lounge of the Peninsula was invaded by a bevy of Mr Marcus' lovelies and peaches. Many a whisky dry was suspended in mid-air." The show opened to packed houses at the Queen's theatre. There were comedy acts, acrobats, dancers, skits, musicians, a contortionist and "silver goddesses dressed only in silver paint". "The whole show is framed to appeal to the eye and the senses rather than to the brain, with gorgeous dresses and lovely legs, so that a knowledge of English is not necessary to its enjoyment."

The celebrities of the era occasionally passed through Hong Kong on world cruises and entertained the local press.

In the early days of flying, aeronautical pioneers made the headlines. One renowned aviatrix provided entertainment for the Hong Kong public in 1932 when she arrived by ship from Japan with her Junkers low-wing monoplane on board. Marga Van Etzdorf had already flown alone from Berlin to Tokyo via Siberia, but she had been unable to fly from Tokyo to Hong Kong because of the war in Manchuria. She nevertheless stirred the imagination of Hong Kong people with stories of how she made a forced landing in the middle of a Siberian winter, got out, repaired the engine and flew off again. There were big crowds to watch her plane being reassembled and tested at Kai Tak and to wave her off on her epic return journey to Berlin.

The Irish playwright and critic, George Bernard Shaw, raised a few eyebrows on a visit to Hong Kong a year later when he told the Hong Kong University Students' Union, "Always argue with your teacher ... If you have a professor of history who gives you his views on history, what you have to say is: 'Now look here, we have heard your views, but what we are going to do is to find another professor of history who disagrees with you.'"

There were other visitors to Hong Kong like the so-called "dope king", "Brilliant" Chang, owner of a West End restaurant which in the twenties had become the centre of a London social set notorious for their fast living. He was met by friends at Kowloon Wharf in May 1925, en route from England to China. Said to be the head of an international drug syndicate, he had attracted wide media attention following his involvement in the Freda Kempton murder case. Miss Kempton, a socialite, had died in mysterious circumstances after attending a Victory Ball at the Albert Hall. Although arrested on suspicion of complicity, he was later released.

A no less newsworthy visitor was the Tibetan lama, Reverend Dr Wongyat. His arrival in July 1935 came shortly after the appointment of a five year old peasant boy as Dalai Lama. The seventy-nine year old head of a monastery of seven thousand monks caused much mirth in Hong Kong, if only inadvertently. Having lived an ascetic life as a lama, he delighted Hong Kong people with the revelation that he had been given a special dispensation to smoke one cigarette every two hours. While in the colony he saw his first film, *Popeye the Sailor*. "Are there really people like that in America?" he asked, to gales of laughter. On the subject of refrigeration: "I knew that electricity made things hot, but this is the first time that I knew it made things cold." On his departure, friends presented him with a fully charged soda siphon – such was the understanding between West and East.

For those who sought entertainment away from the home or the club, there was tea dancing at tea-time and dinner dances and balls in the evening. The Gripps on the first floor of the Hong Kong Hotel, the Rose Room and Roof Garden at the Peninsula and the Repulse Bay Hotel ballroom were the most popular venues.

Dancing generally finished at midnight. Hong Kong, unlike the more international and urbane Shanghai, was not a late-night city. "Everything ended very early in Hong Kong," recalls Peggy Beard. "We were considered terribly dull and staid by Shanghai people as everything had to stop at midnight on Saturday night because of Sunday the next day. It just wasn't considered right to go and enjoy yourself on a Sunday." Nevertheless, dancing had its compensations for sociable young women. "There were masses of young men and very few girls, so we had a super time."

Eric Himsworth danced regularly at the Gripps, but never with a Chinese girl. "Very few Chinese people went to dances and an expat. would never get a dance with a good-class Chinese girl. Of course, you could get a dance with a Suzie Wong type, but you would never take her to the Gripps. The only time you could dance with an upper-class Chinese girl was at Government House. Whenever we fellows went there we wouldn't dance with anybody else. It was the ADC's job to mix the communities at Government House balls, so he would be glad to introduce you. You had to sign up in their programmes but never for more than two dances. But you never asked them for a date because you would never have got one, and anyway, you would cause her embarrassment by having her refuse."

The Raven sisters attended numerous balls at Government House, which they now mostly remember for the great blocks of ice placed around the ballroom: electric fans trained on the blocks of ice served as an early form of air-conditioning in the summer months. Dressing for a ball was a serious and time-consuming business. Dorothy recalls, "Our amah always liked her Missies to be the best-dressed there. She'd iron several dresses for each of us, so we could choose which we wanted. In those days you didn't get crease-resistant materials. They used to crush up like mad."

For girls like Marjorie Angus who worked in Central and wanted to go straight from the office to a tea dance or a ball, the Women's International Club provided an ironing service for crushable dresses.

Before a dance at the Gripps, the men would meet in Bessie's Bar and later join the ladies in the hotel's lounge bar. The gimlet (a mix of gin, lime juice, water and ice) was the most popular pre-war drink for ladies and cost twenty cents a glass in the late twenties. A whisky and soda cost thirty cents and was the most common social drink for men, although cocktails like Side-cars, Bronxes, Manhattans and Angels' Kisses were popular with both sexes.

The practice of having partners sign up dance programmes ensured that everyone enjoyed a full evening's dancing and both sexes could play the field. Peggy Beard's programme was never empty. "You came in with your programme and all the young men were waiting at the door. They put down their names so you were always booked up. They never tried to monopolise you, it wouldn't have been approved of. Besides, Mother wouldn't have approved of having more than two dances with any one partner."

Occasionally, there was an international celebrity on the dance floor. Marjorie Angus was kicked in the shins by Prince George (later the Duke of Kent) at the Repulse Bay Hotel. "He was an awful dancer, all he could do was the Charleston." The prince had come out to Hong Kong aboard HMS *Hawkins* and had gained a reputation of being something of a lad. "He got entangled with a half-Filipina, half-Scottish girl named Anna Birkett (we called her Anna 'Bucket'),the daughter of a judge in Manila. As a Eurasian she was not recognised at Government House. The prince had the reputation of being a heavy drinker at the time. When he left, the single girls lined up to see him go, weeping. We didn't see him, though. He'd been rather the worse for wear, so they'd taken him round to the offside of the ship, wrapped up in a blanket, and hoisted him on board away from the public gaze," remembers Marjorie Angus.

Anna Birkett and her mother apparently

Violet Capell at home in Kowloon, 1925. Violet Capell's dance classes were for years attended by Hong Kong girls. Peggy Beard went to her from the Peak in the twenties, Amina el Arculli attended her classes in the late thirties.

Hongkong Telegraph, 1931. Miss Capell's dancing classes were highly respectable but open to all races. The Select Dance Club was racially exclusive, but rather less respectable.

Violet Capell and her dancing girls, 1925. The girls put on a show at the Queen's. Peggy Beard (fifth from left) remembers tripping across the stage as a tulip to the tune of 'Tiptoe through the Tulips'.

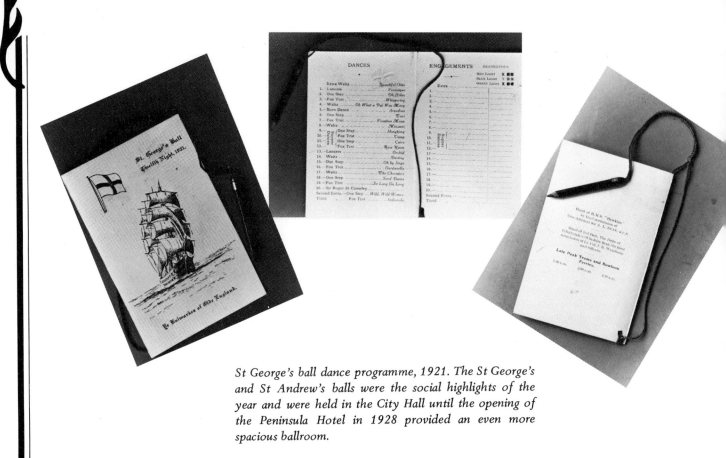

St George's ball dance programme, 1921. The St George's and St Andrew's balls were the social highlights of the year and were held in the City Hall until the opening of the Peninsula Hotel in 1928 provided an even more spacious ballroom.

followed the prince but the British consul at Shanghai asked them to leave the ship, an Empress boat bound for Vancouver. They were taken off and he went home unencumbered. Marjorie Angus recalls that the following year a christening was announced in the social pages of the English press. The baby was named Georgina and the former Anna Birkett, now married to a naval officer, was the mother. "We often wondered how many Georginas there were in Hong Kong."

The main social events of the year were the St George's and St Andrew's balls, which gave the community the opportunity to see and be seen. At the St George's ball held on Twelfth Night 1930, there were eight hundred guests. It was the first time the ball had been held at the new Peninsula Hotel and Twelfth Night, rather than St George's Day, had been chosen because weather conditions were more reminiscent of home. As always, the president of the society

was given the opportunity to sing the praises of England and the English. "The society of St George exists for the purpose of strengthening the sentiment of English nationality . . . St George is representative of individual effort . . . I venture to suggest that St George did not sit on a committee and vote for somebody else to slay dragons."

A company of Beefeaters in full regalia with white beards and enormous halberds formed a guard of honour for the official party led by Sir Cecil and Lady Clementi. As they moved in stately procession up the ballroom, the Somerset Light Infantry struck up 'Roast Beef of Old England'. Around the walls of the two ballrooms used for the event were the crests of English towns and civic flags. Behind the dais where the guests of honour sat was a huge emblem of St George flanked by red and white standards, and half-way through the meal another fanfare heralded the entrance of the boar's head.

Lane, Crawford catalogue, 1926.

Lane, Crawford catalogue, 1933.

After-dinner speeches extolled England. Speakers borrowed from Wordsworth: "I travelled among unknown men/In lands beyond the sea./ England! I never knew till then/The love I bore for thee." And Shakespeare: "This blessed plot this earth, this realm, this England."

For those who refrained from dancing, there was a card room, a ladies' bar and the "Pig and Whistle", which boasted the qualities that had "made the inn so fine and typical a part of English village life". Dance numbers included 'You're the Cream in My Coffee', 'Makin' Whoopee', 'Good Little, Bad Little You' and 'Underneath the Russian Moon'. In all, sixteen foxtrots, five waltzes and one lancers were accomplished by courtesy of the resident Filipino band.

Being a special event it went on well beyond midnight. Special cross-harbour ferries were laid on and the Peak trams ran late to transport the revellers back to their Peak homes.

The Raven sisters were such good dancers that they sometimes performed in charity cabarets at the Hong Kong Hotel and the Peninsula. They had studied acrobatics and tap dancing and had taken ballet lessons with George Gontcharov at his studio in Garden Terrace, Garden Road. Gontcharov, a White Russian emigré who had danced at the Bolshoi before the revolution, had taught Peggy Hookham (Margot Fonteyn) in Shanghai before coming to Hong Kong in the mid-thirties.

The Raven sisters loved going to tea dances on the terrace of the newly opened Repulse Bay Lido or on the roof of the Hong Kong Hotel. "You wore proper afternoon dress and stockings, even in summer. The idea was to waltz, tango, foxtrot or rhumba in between intervals for cups of tea and cream cakes. The dances were between five and seven o'clock and were often a preliminary to a movie show, dinner or fancy dress party. We sometimes went to four tea dances a week if we were invited."

Peggy Hookham formed her first dancing partnership at a tea dance in the Repulse Bay Hotel, where she was staying with her mother on her way back to school in China in 1930. Her partner was a tall Norwegian who had been a diplomat in Russia before the revolution. "At every tea dance in the Repulse Bay Hotel we waltzed and foxtrotted and danced the paso doble, he so tall and me a little shrimp of eleven years, but in perfect harmony. He loved the ballet in St Petersburg and Moscow, knew about all the ballerinas and talked to me for hours on the beach about Tamara Karsavina in *Sleeping Beauty*," she wrote in her autobiography, *Margot Fonteyn*. Years later, when she was dancing in Oslo, she received a letter saying, "I wonder can the famous Margot Fonteyn be the little Peggy I used to know in Hong Kong?" Enclosed was a snapshot of her and the tall Norwegian sitting together on the beach, with the words, "This is Peggy, she swims like a fish and dances like a ballerina, summer 1930" on the back.

During the flapper era of knee-length skirts, silk stockings, headbands and the Charleston, the girls most sought after were those with shapely legs and flat chests. Those unfortunate enough to have well-developed busts were advised by the *Hongkong Telegraph* never to wear shiny fabrics or lamé, as "all ballroom, restaurant and theatre lighting is from above, highlighting the upper body and thus emphasising the bust". It was

suggested they should wear cardigans by day and loose lace jackets for evening wear.

In the thirties shy women could hide behind a fan, which came into fashion after Hollywood stars and Parisian *couturiers* had transformed the Chinese accessory into one acceptable to Western women. The *South China Morning Post* advised its female readers in 1938 that "The fan in the hands of the uninitiated is like a good actor minus a role," and went on to explain how to master its subtle language. Clasped lightly in the hand and waved languidly it meant, "I am fatigued and would like refreshment and gallant care." Waved quickly, with agitation, it meant, "Something has annoyed me. I need to be calmed down. Please do not argue." Held closed and tapped lightly, but coquettishly, on the arm of a partner signalled an admonitory mood, demanding undivided attention. Folded demurely and clasped with both hands in the lap, the owner's eyes averted, meant "rather shy but willing to try".

Thus the colony fanned, danced, sang, drank and played its way through the Charleston era and into the next. After the general strike and boycott there was little to disturb the tempo of life for Europeans in Hong Kong. Only when war clouds began to gather over China and Europe was there the slightest presentiment that the pleasures of living in Hong Kong might not last forever.

THE SPORTING LIFE

"It was said, not without some grain of truth, that if you wanted service at the Hongkong and Shanghai Bank you had to be wearing your Cricket Club tie."

Michael Wright

Social life for most expatriates in pre-war Hong Kong revolved around home and the club. Not one club, but many. With no waiting lists and low entry fees, membership of half a dozen clubs was common as long as one passed muster and was accepted as the right sort of person.

Eric Himsworth was typical of many young sportsmen. After arriving in Hong Kong in 1929, he quickly became a member of the Civil Service, Cricket, Yacht, Football, Victoria Rowing and Shatin Riding Clubs. Not the Hong Kong Club, of course: he was far too young for that. "You do not consider the Hong Kong Club," he was told on his arrival "They wouldn't look at a whipper-snapper like you."

Fees at most clubs were well within the reach of a young professional. Michael Wright, who returned to Hong Kong in the late thirties, remembers paying three dollars a month for membership of the Cricket Club and five dollars for the Golf Club.

Not all expatriates, however, were welcome. "I knew a clerk of works who failed to get into the Hong Kong Cricket Club even though he once played first-class cricket for Lancashire," Michael Wright recalls. Wright himself was accepted, however, being a professional with paid first-class passage on the P & O. Those with second-class P & O passages did not make the grade.

Not all clubs were as fussy. The Craigengower Cricket Club paved the way as a democratic and multi-racial club on the island, while the Kowloon Cricket Club allowed in Chinese, Eurasians and English clerks of works well ahead of most island clubs. The Chinese also had the South China Recreation Club and the North Point Swimming Club and the Indians and the Portuguese had clubs of their own.

The tempo of expatriate life in pre-war Hong Kong was much more leisurely than it is today. A spurt of feverish activity to get business done followed the arrival of incoming mail, but then there was a lull until the next mail steamer came in. As Michael Wright remembers, "There just wasn't any pressure before the war so you tended to drink quite a bit at lunchtime and then knock off at three or so for a game of hockey or cricket." The Cricket Club was the mecca for the European business community as it was so close to Central offices. Leslie Ralph recalls jumping into a rickshaw outside the Union Insurance office and being on the cricket pitch in his whites by 5.15 every evening of the cricket season. It was generally accepted that if a young man were intending to follow pursuits as healthy and gentlemanly as hockey or cricket, it was only right he should be given time off work in which to indulge in them.

Sportsmen could turn their hand to something different every evening: cricket at the Cricket Club, badminton at the Peak Club, tennis at the Ladies' Recreation Club, rowing from the Victoria Rowing Club opposite Statue Square and sailing from the Yacht Club on Kellett Island.

Hong Kong Hockey Club, 1931. This picture was taken before the club's defeat of the Navy team in March 1931.

Lane, Crawford catalogue, 1933.

Lane, Crawford catalogue, 1933.

Hong Kong versus Shanghai interport match, 1931.

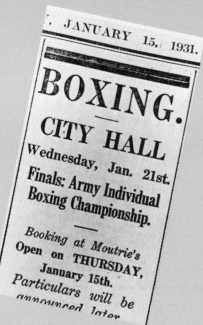

South China Morning Post, *1931.*

Ladies' hockey team, Kowloon, mid-twenties. The ladies' hockey team was all-English. Marjorie Angus (first left, back row), who played in goal, claims that the team had difficulty finding suitable opponents at first and had to play against Indian regiments or sailors off the ship. This team won the coveted Clare Cup three years running.

Anyone for tennis? Kowloon, 1928.

Houses on the Peak often had tennis courts, so there were numerous tennis parties ("Not very good tennis, but lovely parties"). In winter, rugger, hockey and soccer matches were organised. In the middle of Happy Valley there was a nine-hole golf course, so it was possible to get in a round of golf after office hours and be home for tea.

Leslie Ralph's favourite sport was riding at Happy Valley. In those days jockeys were gentlemen amateurs who rode for fun. "I left the mess at 114 The Peak at 5.30 a.m. and freewheeled on my bicycle down to the racecourse. It was a point of honour with me that I didn't pedal more than two or three times all the way to Happy Valley. I then rode some ponies, changed, had breakfast and was in the office by 8.30 a.m. My bike was pushed back up the Peak by a coolie, whom I paid fifty cents a day."

His claim to local fame came one day in November 1927 when he rode five winners for one owner, an all-time record win for one owner in one day. "All I had that day was a glass of champagne between each of the five races. Afterwards we had a bit of a party at the mess, the result of which was that we had to repaint the walls of the dining room."

North China or Mongolian ponies were used at Happy Valley in those days. "You had to sit low in the saddle and lift them along with your legs down. You helped the pony with your body, which was much more strenuous than riding short. Later, Australian ponies were used and had to be ridden short, or 'high up' so that your weight would be off the horse." Leslie Ralph was fortunate as he had learned to ride short in India. Some of the best jockeys came from Shanghai, mainly Europeans from the international settlement or emigré White Russians who had come to China after the revolution.

Harry Esmail remembers the Shanghai jockeys riding in the annual four-day racing jamborees at the valley. "There was gambling — not for big stakes in those days, but mainly for fun. It was like a four-day festival. There were stalls selling all sorts of food, kids were in their Sunday best and all Hong Kong seemed to be there. It was like carnival time."

Other equestrian activities on the island included polo at Causeway Bay and the annual gymkhanas, organised by the Volunteers, held on the polo ground. Riding competitions, "tent-pegging" (in which riders with long spears galloped at tent-pegs in a simulation of the Indian sport of pig-sticking) and pony rides for children were among the events. The polo ground was specially decorated for the annual occasion, music was provided by a regimental band and the whole expatriate community was invariably there.

There was also a thriving Cycling Club. The building of new roads opened up hitherto unvisited routes around the colony and the relative absence of motor traffic made cycling a pleasure. The doyen of Hong Kong's cyclists was H.A.G. Keats, the club's president and the colony champion in the late thirties, whose record of 2 hours, 38 minutes, 15 seconds over fifty miles seemed unbeatable at the time. One Christmas the club organised a three hundred mile tour into China which was, however, only taken up by three of the club's Chinese members; presumably, the prospect of cycling for six days over Yuletide was too daunting even for H.A.G. Keats.

Happy Valley, 1925.

Leslie Ralph's five winners with mafoos, Happy Valley, 28 February 1927. Leslie Ralph's copy of this photograph showing his winning mounts — The Geezer, The Gnome, The Gomeril, The Goblin and Saligia — was lost in the Japanese occupation. This copy hung on the wall of Hall and Shenton's box at the Jockey Club and was preserved through the war years by one of the mafoos in the photograph. Mrs Hall sent it to Leslie Ralph on the death of her husband.

Mrs Dunbar leading in Fortune Bay, Mr Hill up, 1931.

Punters at the annual four-day meeting at Happy Valley, 1931.

The grandstand at Happy Valley, 1937.

Captain Alec Hutton Potts "tent-pegging".

Programme
of events.

Gymkhana at the polo ground,
Causeway Bay, 1932.

VIP tent.

Most forms of sport, however, were closed to the majority of those living in Hong Kong. Insufficient provision for Chinese youth to play sports was thought to be one of the reasons for the high level of opium addiction. Nevertheless, for those Chinese who were able to take advantage of the facilities which did exist — and the opium commission of 1935 replied to the government's critics by referring to the fourteen acres given over to Chinese recreation clubs — there was the chance to meet Europeans in equal combat on the playing field. In 1935, for example, all the senior football trophies and the colony's league championship were held by Chinese clubs.

The beaches of Hong Kong, relatively unspoiled and unpolluted before the war, were generally regarded as the sole province of the expatriates. The majority of the Chinese had neither the time nor the money to get out to the beaches, and it was unheard of for Chinese girls to be seen in public in bathing costumes. There was also a strong feeling among Europeans that the beaches were out of bounds to Chinese people, who were largely confined to one swimming area, a sea-bathing club off North Point.

As the urban area of Hong Kong was limited with industry on a small scale, the water around Hong Kong was fairly clear and clean. There were beaches in places that would seem inconceivable today — North Point, Kennedy Town and Hunghom — but the favourites were Repulse Bay, Stanley, Deepwater and Big Wave Bays. Until the road was built out to the south side of the island in the early 1920s, access to Repulse Bay beach and those beyond was by motor launch. Before the vehicular ferry was opened in 1935, Kowloon residents would motor out to Castle Peak beach rather than cross over to the island.

*Winter beach picnic, Castle Peak,
late twenties.*

*Marjorie Angus and Kowloon friends
on Castle Peak beach, late twenties.*

68

Hong Kong and Shanghai Hotels, which owned the Hong Kong and Peak Hotels, opened the Repulse Bay Hotel to serve the southern part of the island in 1919.

Motor cars in the car park of the Repulse Bay Hotel at the time of its opening, 1919. The trip from the hotel to Central took an hour until the opening of Wongneichong Gap Road in the early thirties considerably reduced the time. The large structure in the bay was used as a landing stage for flying boats on the Hong Kong-Macau run.

Repulse Bay beach, 1927.

Repulse Bay beach, 1926. Never crowded, even on summer weekends, Repulse Bay became the most popular beach in the colony after the road to Repulse Bay was opened in 1919.

Repulse Bay Hotel with direct access to the beach, 1927.

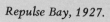
Repulse Bay, 1927.

The Repulse Bay Lido, 1938.

On the steps of a Repulse Bay matshed, 1927.

Girl in beach pyjamas, 1933. In the days when it was considered dangerous to get too much sun, paper umbrellas were popular as beach parasols.

Tiffin inside a Repulse Bay matshed, 1927. Matsheds were also used by wives in the daytime for bridge and mah-jong sessions.

Repulse Bay seen from above Eucliffe, 1938. Deprived of the chance to live on the Peak, wealthy Chinese business-men built their mansions elsewhere. Both Eucliffe and Euston (in Bonham Road) were built by millionaire Eu Ton-sen.

A feature of the main beaches was the matshed, a large bamboo structure with roof and walls of rush matting and palm fronds which served as a beach house. All the big firms had them and individuals either bought or hired them for use as changing rooms, picnic places, retreats from the sun or rain or for rendezvous after dark. With journeys back to England few and far between, it was essential to make the most of Hong Kong beaches and having a matshed gave people a sense of permanence. There were 120 licensed matsheds on Repulse Bay beach, making it easily the most popular beach in the whole territory. The next most popular beach was Castle Peak with twenty-eight matsheds on it. Stanley Bay beach had only five and there were none at Deepwater Bay due to

the proximity of the road at high tide. Matsheds were, of course, vulnerable to typhoons, and it cost seventy-five dollars to have one re-erected.

There was plenty of room on Repulse Bay beach even on a Saturday afternoon at the height of the swimming season. Beach picnics were a favourite pastime and, as there were no fast-food places, people took their own food in picnic hampers packed by the houseboy. On the matshed verandah, families and friends would tuck into delicacies from Lane, Crawford and wine provided by the local compadore.

The Repulse Bay Hotel was a favourite honey-moon spot. Marjorie Angus recalls spending her honeymoon there after her wedding at St Andrew's Church, Kowloon, on 4 June 1934.

"We had five meals a day; early morning tea, a huge breakfast, tiffin, afternoon tea, dinner, all for nine dollars a day each. We played tennis and swam and my husband played golf at Deepwater Bay. There was a dinner dance on the Saturday night and tea dances on Sunday afternoons. There was a regular hotel bus going into Victoria which you could take for twenty cents. It stopped off at the Hong Kong Hotel in Pedder Street and, after a morning's shopping, you could have lunch there before returning to Repulse Bay."

An added attraction to Repulse Bay beach was the Lido which opened as a restaurant and venue for afternoon tea dances in 1937. All was not perfect at Repulse Bay, however. A report on the beach recommended the following improvements: that the litter problem be dealt with by cutting down the undergrowth surrounding the matsheds; that the smell from the stagnant pool at the west end be removed by drainage; that the rocks and boulders which spoiled the eastern half of the beach be taken away; that two sets of toilets be built at either end of the beach; and that the stream running down the middle of the beach be channelled down to the water mark. Nor was the beach entirely quiet and peaceful, as the bay was used as a seaport by flying boats.

The most convenient beach for the office district of Victoria was Stonecutters Island. A steam launch left Blake Pier at five o'clock every evening filled with lawyers, stockbrokers, bankers and secretaries. After a dip in the sea off Stonecutters, office workers would be back home in time for dinner.

There were also launch picnics. Launches were single-funnelled steamboats and could be rented for the day, the evening or the weekend. In the days before waterskiing, a favourite sport was aquaplaning, which involved being pulled along on a board attached to the launch by a rope.

Aquaplaning, 1927.

Behaviour on these occasions was very proper. There was never any question of young people spending the night at a matshed or on a launch. Peggy Beard's mother did not approve of her having more than two late nights a week at the age of nineteen. "I had my twenty-first birthday party at the Shek-O Club. After that, I was allowed to go on launch or beach picnics with a bunch of people, never singly. There always had to be one married woman in the party to act as a chaperone."

As most European children were sent away to boarding school, there were few of them on the beaches of Hong Kong. Michael Wright did spend his earliest years in Hong Kong and remembers his parents being worried about sun-stroke. "We children always wore great big topees in the sun. We even had to wear a topee on the beach. In the water we were allowed to take the topee off on condition that every five minutes we ducked our heads to keep our hair wet. After a swim the grown-ups had cherry brandy to warm themselves up. We kids were given a sip too. So bathing picnics for me meant topees and cherry brandy."

Big Wave Bay, 1920. Residents of Shek-O had the run of Big Wave Bay and Shek-O beaches, which were as deserted at weekends as they were during the week.

The Shek-O Club and members, late twenties. A group of people who thought it would be a good idea to live in the country and escape the fogs of the Peak set up the Shek-O Development Company in the early twenties to develop the area for European settlement. Peggy Beard's father, Lennox Godfrey Bird, and uncle, who were partners in the architectural firm of Palmer and Turner (formerly Bird and Palmer), built the first bungalows and the Shek-O Club in 1925.

Bird's bungalow, Shek-O, 1932. Jean Bird, Peggy Beard's sister, had this windsock put up in the garden so that boyfriends stationed at Kai Tak could drop letters to her from their flying boats.

Mit, Jean Bird, Peggy Beard, Lennox Godfrey Bird, Kenneth Beard and young John Beard enjoy a pre-lunch Christmas drink at the family bungalow in Shek-O in 1932. Jean's boyfriend, a member of the well-known Mitford family, was a submarine lieutenant.

Shenton's bungalow, Shek-O, 1932. Post was picked up from the clubhouse, so there was no need to number the bungalows, which were known by the owners' names. Lennox Godfrey Bird designed the bungalow with a Chinese-style roof which, he believed, would better withstand typhoons.

9

COOLIE LIFE

"The Chinese peasant works long hours for a scanty wage and gets practically no holidays. In general, the Chinese are inclined to be fatalists. Although this attitude facilitates the government of the masses, it is unfortunately inimical to progress. Contact with Europeans is bound, in the course of time, to have some effect on the character of those who make Hong Kong their home."

Housing report, 1935

The Chinese coolie class formed the basis of Hong Kong's population between the wars. Working insufferably long hours for wages which barely kept them alive, coolies ate little and were susceptible to disease. Their homes were bed-spaces in overcrowded, filthy tenement buildings. Their clothing was minimal and they usually went without shoes, prompting Bob Yates, a British soldier stationed in Hong Kong in the late thirties, to remark, "If you saw a Chinaman in a pair of shoes you wondered where he'd pinched them from."

To escape their misery they smoked black-market adulterated opium in seedy little divans and suffered the consequences in bad physical and mental health. Racked by a life of hard physical work from early childhood, poor diet and in many cases the effects of too much opium, their lives were short. Corpses of the destitute were left in the streets to be collected by other coolies on handcarts and accorded a pauper's burial.

A few, admittedly, moved up in society to become rich and powerful, or simply well-to-do, but the odds against this were high. Charitable organisations existed to help those unable to cope with the struggle for survival, but the general ethos of Hong Kong's *laissez-faire* capitalism worked in favour of the rich.

The lives of the rich and famous, like Sir Robert Ho-tung or Sir Paul Chater, are well documented, but only occasionally can one catch a glimpse of coolies as individuals. In 1939 Hong Kong's labour officer interviewed twenty coolies found on the colony's streets. He chose them at random. Of the twenty only one was born in Hong Kong.

Yiu Sun was buying his daily quota of six cigarettes for three cents from a stall in Hing Lung Street when he was approached by the interviewer. He had arrived in Hong Kong the year before, having left the smallholding he farmed in his native village of Kung Moon to find more lucrative work in Hong Kong. Upon arriving in the colony, a clansman introduced him to a coolie foreman employed by the tea guild and he was given a job carrying tea chests for a shipping company at five dollars a week. On days when there were no tea ships in the harbour he carried vegetables to Central market at the rate of seventy cents a day. He had been married for four years and had left his wife with his mother, both of whom he was helping to support by sending home ten dollars a month. He shared a cockloft with

two other workers in a tenement building at 10 Chinese Street for a dollar a month. In the same first-floor flat lived eighteen other adults and six children. He ate two twenty-cent meals a day at a cooked-food stall. If he were sick, a female relative married to a coolie living on the same street looked after him. He could neither read nor write, but a clansman wrote letters home for him twice a month and a travelling trader on a Kung Moon boat delivered his remittances, after changing them into Chinese currency.

He worked from eight in the morning until nine at night with Sundays off. Since coming to Hong Kong he had given up worshipping the gods he had revered at home. He wore the clothes he had brought with him from China, but never wore shoes. For the winter he had two singlets, two old jackets and two pairs of trousers. He said he did not gamble or smoke opium, but spent three cents a day on six cigarettes and five cents a day on wine.

Sixty year old Lam Yee was hawking peanuts on Connaught Road. She had come to Hong Kong from Kwangtung fifteen years before as a street seamstress, but became an unlicensed hawker when her sight failed. She had left Canton with her two children after the death of her husband, as his family had refused to take her in. She now heard nothing from her son, who had emigrated to an unknown destination, and presumed that he had been kidnapped. Her daughter had married into a family in the country, but she had not heard from her for a year. Her home was a bed-space in a flat shared with five other families in Des Voeux Road West. The tenant had taken pity on her so she paid no fixed rent. She earned fifteen cents a day hawking peanuts and lived on two meals of rice, salted fish and vegetables, which cost her ten cents a day. She had been arrested twice for hawking without a licence and the fines of fifty cents had finished her capital. The clothes she wore were ten years old. She was seldom sick and felt that life was wonderful in Hong Kong compared to the country.

Twenty-two year old Cheng Kwai-ying worked in a rubber shoe factory in Shaukeiwan. Unmarried, she shared a flat with a brother and sister-in-law and twenty other people. She earned seventy cents a day stretching uppers on fifty pairs of shoes and supplemented her income with some sewing, having bought her own sewing machine second-hand. She worked fourteen hours a day, seven days a week, but was better off in Hong Kong than she had been as a worker in a silk factory in Canton. She was unable to read or write, but very occasionally went to the cinema, her only form of leisure.

Thirty-one year old Cheng Yaw-lim was married to an unemployed seaman and lived in a cubicle in Shamshuipo. To support three young children, she worked in a Kowloon factory wrapping paper around manganese torch batteries. For a twelve-hour day her wages were twenty-one cents and she had no day off. The oldest child, a boy of eleven, did the family cooking.

According to the colony's assessor, the average rent for a single bedspace in 1939 was $2.50 to $3.00 a month and $5.00 to $6.00 for a cubicle in a coolie tenement house. He estimated that the monthly food cost was $5.50 for a single man, or about $15.00 for a couple with two small children. A coolie job with the government provided the satisfaction of job security, but little income. The starting salary for coolies in government service in 1939 was thirteen dollars a month, though scavenging coolies earned a dollar less. Third-class postmen started at seventeen dollars a month, while railway porters and gatemen started at thirteen dollars. Rickshaw coolies could make twenty dollars a month if they worked flat out without a day off, while coal coolies could manage sixteen dollars if they worked the same hours. Tram drivers, on the other hand, could make up to forty-five dollars at the top of the scale, and bus drivers could go as high as fifty-five dollars.

On average, skilled workers in Hong Kong in the late thirties made between thirty and seventy dollars a month, while unskilled workers earned anything between fifteen and twenty-four dollars a month. Most workers, however, were unskilled casual labourers, whose joint income, if they were married, was generally between fourteen and thirty dollars a month. A housing report for 1935 recognised that the lot of the ordinary coolie living and working in Hong Kong was an unenviable one.

After the outbreak of the Sino-Japanese War in 1937 the cost of firewood increased so much that it became cheaper to eat at a cooked-food stall than to cook at home, which led to an increase in the incidence of beriberi and typhoid in the colony. With the high price of cow's milk, children were generally suckled until they were old enough to digest rice. The Hong Kong Eugenics League estimated in 1939 that the infant mortality rate in the colony was 345, compared with fifty-eight in Britain and thirty-eight in Sweden, although it was lower than in most Asian countries.

The league existed to promote birth control, but faced a major problem with the outbreak of war in Europe when their supply of diaphragms from England was stopped. They later discovered a new source of cheaper diaphragms in New York. The league dealt with women like one forty-four year old coolie who was having her fifteenth pregnancy. She had seven children, one of whom she had given away, and was married to a coolie whose take-home pay was five dollars a month until he became unemployed. The husband had been taking Chinese pills to make himself sterile, but to no effect. The woman was referred to the league in a desperate state after she had unsuccessfully tried to give herself an abortion by drinking a concoction of wild flowers boiled with rusty nails, putrefied eggs and urine.

The government did little to help the plight of the poor in spite of recognising how desperately they needed assistance. An administration report of 1939 stated, "It must be admitted that the majority of the colony's working class exist under deplorable conditions at rates of pay which can hardly be regarded as a 'living wage'. For example, one contractor employing several hundred coolies, on being asked what the sick rate was, said there was none, as all sick coolies were dismissed."

The sub-contracting system was blamed as a major cause of low pay. In the building industry the situation was especially bad. A contract sublet through several intermediaries would result in the actual contractor who did the work receiving so little that he would go bankrupt if he did not grossly underpay his labourers. Other sub-contractors charged very high commissions. A petition by Kowloon rickshaw coolies complained that sub-contractors who themselves hired rickshaws for forty-five to fifty cents a day were subletting them to the actual pullers at the inflated rate of seventy-five to eighty cents a day.

The so-called "apprenticeship system" was considered an evil by coolies and government alike. Employers would demand several years' apprenticeship in an unskilled trade which could be mastered in weeks. It was an excuse for obtaining cheap labour and was equated with the mui-tsai system for girls. The practice was not confined to the sweat shops of the city, but extended to domestic labour on the Peak, where a cook might require a long apprenticeship from a "makee learn" boy, who would end up doing most of the work for half the pay.

Hong Kong could always fall back on its low unemployment figures in a world facing the post-Wall Street crash depression. The statistics, however, were largely the result of many men doing the work of one. The plumber's mate, for instance, swelled into a gang of assistants, most of whom stood around doing nothing, so that instead of one man drawing a reasonable wage, a number of men would be taking home barely enough to live on.

Most factories in Hong Kong were converted tenements. Of the twelve thousand factories in Kowloon in 1939, over a thousand were housed in tenements, with no provision for toilets, eating areas, safety regulations or first-aid. The worst conditions were found in knitting factories, which were in direct competition with similar factories

Coolie women on construction work, 1939. Heavy work on building and reclamation sites was often done by women in the days before bulldozers and dump trucks. Hillsides were literally demolished bucket by bucket by Hong Kong's coolie women.

Coolie boy, 1937. The fashion for very young boys was to have the head shaved, leaving a small lump of hair above the forehead so that they could be "lifted up to heaven and saved from the sea".

Tourist:—"Say, Ma; he was probably a Hongkong bullion-broker at one time!"

The effects of the depression on Hong Kong, South China Morning Post, 1932.

Coolie children, 1937. Many children like these worked the streets as messengers and newspaper sellers for a few cents a day.

in China. They mainly employed women, who earned between fifteen and twenty cents for a day which began at 7.00 a.m. and ended at 5.00 p.m. Most worked overtime until 9.00 p.m. at the same rate.

There were exceptions. The Hong Kong Brewery provided a fair wage and adequate housing for its employees, with hot and cold baths, and the Hume Pipe Company in Tsuen Wan was modelled on an English garden suburb, but such enlightened management was very much the exception.

The government's attitude to social reform was one of extreme caution, as summed up in the economic commission report of 1936. "Social reforms based on Western models should only be introduced into Hong Kong in reasonable conformity with those enforced in neighbouring countries. The introduction of legislation for the betterment of working conditions should be cautious and not over-ambitious, lest it defeat itself."

The fact of the matter was that working conditions in neighbouring countries were even worse than in Hong Kong, and the government felt that, if the lot of the Chinese worker were improved, the refugee influx into the colony would become insupportable.

In one area, however, the government had made some advances by the late thirties. Child labour in Hong Kong factories had been more or less eliminated following the recommendations of the 1921 Commission on Conditions of the Industrial Employment of Children. The commission made some shocking revelations which could not be ignored: Mongkok factory girls aged eleven working up to ninety-six hours a week including night shifts; boys employed in dockyards as boiler-chippers because grown men were too big to climb into boiler manholes; boys blowing glass in front of hot furnaces from six in the morning until eleven at night in an atmosphere filled with noxious gases and floating glass particles, for a dollar a month plus food; children being blown up in unsafe firecracker factories. Child labour was so cheap that at the

age of sixteen children were often sacked, to be replaced by younger ones. The most easily dispensed with were those whose health and spirit had been broken by the long hours and inhuman working conditions.

Many arguments in support of child labour in the Hong Kong of the early twenties were identical to those voiced at the time of the factory acts in Britain in the 1840s; namely, that children liked working and that families could not survive without their income. Sir Chow Shou-son, like many Chinese businessmen, took a similar line to the one he held over the mui-tsai issue: child labour was Chinese practice and served to protect poor families reliant on the income of all their members.

Conservative opposition notwithstanding, the commission's recommendations led to the 1922 Industrial Employment of Children Ordinance. Its terms forbade the employment of children under fifteen in "dangerous trades" and under ten in other factories. Hours were limited to nine a day, with one day off a week, and no child was allowed to carry a load amounting to anything over forty catties (seventy pounds). Meagre as such a reform might seem by Western and modern standards it was, nevertheless, the first legislative step taken to protect factory workers in the Far East.

Tenement housing in the main coolie districts of Western, Eastern, Yaumatei and Shamshuipo had grown haphazardly from the earliest days of the colony. There was no overall planning and little government intervention, and the large refugee influx resulting from the troubles in China during the twenties and thirties put an intolerable strain on the already overcrowded living conditions of the coolie areas.

The standard width of tenement buildings was based on the traditional "Chinese fir-pole" measurement of thirteen and a half feet. While this was suitable for traditional village houses in south China it was entirely inadequate for three- and four-storey buildings in Hong Kong. By the interwar period most had degenerated into dark and dingy slums, with no flush toilets and only one latrine on the ground floor to serve the whole building. Rooms were divided into cubicles, with inner ones closed off to light and air. The occupants of inner cubicles often had no say in the opening and closing of windows, and it was the customary practice of Chinese slum-dwellers to keep all windows closed whatever the weather. Most were unable to afford electricity, gas or coal, so cooking was done over wood-burning chatties with inadequate ventilation, leaving walls thick with black soot and grime and posing a major fire hazard. Rubbish disposal was inadequate, and trash bins were filled to overflowing, leaving a trail of debris in stairways and streets for the consumption of rats, cockroaches and dogs.

Overpopulation and low wages, together with greedy landlordism, led to an intricate system of subletting. J.H. Seth, the absentee landlord of 55 Hollywood Road, was typical of many who sublet their properties for maximum profit. In 1924 he sublet his dilapidated tenement building to a principal tenant, who in turn sublet flats to a second tier of people, who then let out cubicles and bunks to as many as could crowd into them. A single flat might have up to twenty-five people living in its bedspaces and cocklofts, but with the massive influx of refugees following the outbreak of the Sino-Japanese War the number was sometimes doubled. Partitions separating the cubicles provided little privacy.

Nevertheless, there was a community spirit in such buildings which the privations of life and the overcrowding did nothing to diminish. Kwong Hon Toy Building off Aberdeen Street in the Chinese central district of Hong Kong Island is one of the fast disappearing pre-war tenements still standing in Hong Kong. Less than a mile from

Kwong Hon Toy Building, Central district, 1983.

the downtown highrises of the Central business district, chickens roam the forecourt of Kwong Hon Toy and nightsoil coolies collect its human waste in plastic buckets. Among those living there now are a former rickshaw coolie and opium addict, two young drug addicts, a gangster chief and a number of old widows. One of the widows, seventy-nine year old Mrs Huan, has been living in her cubicle since the early thirties. She, like the others, would never move out and it is not only the low rents which keep her there. What she values most about the building is its community spirit. She is acquainted with practically everybody in the building and whenever she needs assistance there is always a helping hand. She knows, as she did as a young woman in the thirties, that when she feels lonely there is always somebody to talk to.

10

GETTING AROUND

Rickshaw coolies do not, on the whole, lead so hard a life as one might imagine, judging from their general air of contentment and the amount of laughter and badinage that goes on among themselves whilst awaiting fares. After all, the rickshaw is very easy to pull and is only used on level districts, whilst the average distance covered on each journey is a very short one."

Guide book, 1930s

Alexander Grantham, a young cadet in government service in the 1920s who later rose to be governor, described going to a party in Kowloon from his home on the Peak. The journey involved taking a sedan chair to the Peak Tram, descending on the tram, transferring to a second chair for the ride to the Star Ferry terminal, crossing the harbour on a ferry and taking a rickshaw to his final destination. Such a journey took time, but time was plentiful in those days and speed was determined by the strength and stamina of rickshaw pullers and chair bearers.

Rickshaws plied the flat areas, sedan chairs the hills. For less than a dollar one could take a chair from the bottom of Wyndham Street to the top of the Peak, but the normal way of getting home to the Peak was to take a chair along Battery Path to the Peak Tram terminus for twenty cents, transfer to the tram, then take either a rickshaw or a chair to the house. Marjorie Angus remembers the chairs queuing up in Wyndham Street. "Chairs were on one side, with their green mackintosh curtains in case of rain, flower stalls on the other side. If the chair coolies didn't get in step, it was a rough ride. Four bearers were needed if the passenger was a heavyweight. The bamboo poles would creak under the strain, but never give way!"

Peggy Beard recalls travelling to the family's bungalow in Shek-O before the road ran all the way. "The road went as far as where the quarry is now. Mother and I were taken up in chairs over the hill and down the other side. The men walked." When she travelled to a friend's family bungalow in Fanling, she took the train to Fanling station, then a rickshaw the rest of the way.

Taipans on the Peak had their own private chairs and a staff of chair coolies dressed in colourful livery. Peggy's parents had a chair each, but their coolies did not wear uniforms. "They had as little on as possible as they got so hot, poor things."

Eric Himsworth used to watch Peak children being taken to school in family chairs. "It used to turn my stomach to see those kids turn on the bearers with the order, 'Put me down,' then get out and play, then order, 'Pick me up.'"

Bullion and exchange brokers in Ice House Street dashed between banks in company rickshaws with highly polished brasswork trim and low seats designed for getting speedily in and out. Francis Zimmern recalls that in 1941 the Hong Kong Stock Exchange had only six telephones for sixty brokers, a fact which made rickshaws essential.

Sedan chair in Queen's Road East. A great advantage of the chair was that its use need not be confined to roads: passengers who were sick or especially lazy could be carried right on to their verandahs and even into their drawing rooms. However, the swaying motion of chair travel made it inadvisable for those who suffered from travel sickness.

Rickshaw coolies waiting for business on the Praya, 1937.

Rickshaw coolie in Queen's Road East, 1939. Rickshaws were a Japanese import of the late 1870s and were first known as "jinrickishas". In 1939 a rickshaw coolie rented his machine from its owner at twenty cents a day and was lucky if he made a dollar a day.

The majority of residents and visitors seemed to have few reservations about the system. To residents it was the natural order of things and to visitors it was a quaint anachronism. However, a 1930s guide book to Hong Kong reflects mild stirrings of conscience: "Sedan chairs remind one of the England of the seventeenth and eighteenth centuries, and the unapprised visitor looks on them as a curiosity. The Hong Kong resident, however, soon becomes accustomed to both the sight and use of these handy conveyances. Very few big cities have such steep gradients as Hong Kong has, and in summer when the shade temperature is ninety degrees and the humidity over eighty per cent, one, no matter how independent, humane, or communistic he may be, is fain to drop into one of these chairs and lie back limply while the perspiring coolies convey him to the Mid-levels."

Most rickshaw coolies had come into the work from the harsh labour of the Canton countryside. Fifty-seven year old Lau San, for instance, was used to a hard life. Found plying for hire on Connaught Road in 1939, he started work at five in the morning and handed over his rickshaw to a night coolie at five o'clock in the evening. Home was on the third floor of a coolie lodging house, which he shared with thirteen others. They divided the seventeen dollars a month rent between them. Lau San made between seventy cents and a dollar a day, out of which he had to pay twenty cents for the hire of his rickshaw and any repairs. He managed to send six dollars a month to his son in China, who was too poor to marry.

How such men felt about their work goes unrecorded, but in 1924 a number of rickshaw and sedan coolies working on the Peak went on strike. The immediate cause was a police order that they show their licences, in response to which the coolies went to their rest quarters to get them but failed to return. The police replied by applying pressure to the syndicate which owned the rickshaws, and the coolies were back at work within two hours, their attempt at industrial action having come to nothing.

A visiting Shanghai traffic expert later drew attention to the role of the rickshaw puller in 1930 when he criticised the use of rickshaws as "a traffic hazard and a sign of moral backwardness". As a modernist, he also applauded the decision to introduce a vehicular ferry across the harbour, even though there were only five thousand cars in Hong Kong at the time, and suggested that the noisy trams be replaced by railless trolley buses as in Europe. The trams, however, were cheap and convenient. Running between Kennedy Town and Shaukeiwan, they were the sole means of transport for the coolie class before buses appeared in the early 1930s. A tram ride was much cheaper than a ride in a rickshaw.

Trams were the main means of transport for the coolie class as they were much cheaper than rickshaws. Tourists could also enjoy the "only double-deck tramcars in Asia".

Crossing the harbour with a car before the advent of the vehicular ferry service in 1939 was a major operation. Inconvenient as it was, Eric Himsworth remembers the procedure with affection: "If it was a weekday you rang up Star Ferry and ordered a ferry at a given time. They would send across a lighter, which would come alongside the Praya wall just in front of where the Cable & Wireless office is (between Star Ferry and the naval dockyard). The lighter

TO VICTORIA PEAK

This is by far the most important item in the Sightseeing Programme of Hongkong, and the trip by the Funicular Railway (San-teng-fo-chair), St. John's Place Station, Garden Road (only seven minutes from Blake Pier or the Hongkong Hotel), should be made the very first opportunity.

From the flag staff or the Umbrella seat a magnificent view of the harbour with its wonderful shipping and countless sampans, of Kowloon and the hills beyond, can be obtained—The view on a clear night is one which will never be forgotten reminding one as it does of another firmament with more stars in it than in a similar space above.

The unsurpassed panorama to the south dotted with islands as far as the eye can reach can be seen from many vantage points.

Two hours cannot be better spent than visiting the Peak District.

(1825 feet above Sea.)   *(1825 feet above Sea.)*

The time occupied on the ascent is eight minutes, and cars run every ten minutes or quarter-of-an-hour throughout the day, and every half-hour between 8.45 p.m. and 11.45 p.m.

Special cars can be obtained by arrangement at the PEAK TRAMWAY COMPANY'S OFFICE, ALEXANDRA BUILDING.

JOHN D. HUMPHREYS & SON,
General Managers.

Peak Tram, 1937. The opening of the Peak Tram in 1888 made the Peak accessible and stimulated European settlement there.

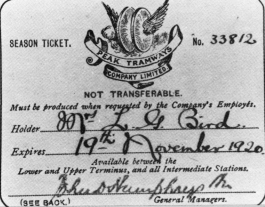

Lennox Godfrey Bird was colonel of the Volunteers. There were distinct class divisions on the tram: first class at the front, second class in the middle and coolie class at the back.

THE "STAR" FERRY COMPANY, LTD.

The easiest, quickest, safest and best way to get to the CITY of VICTORIA, HONGKONG, is by the "STAR" FERRY SERVICE, from their pier immediately adjoining the KOWLOON WHARVES.

PASSENGERS arriving by Mail or other Steamers at any time beween 5.20 a.m. and midnight are always sure of being able to cross the harbour by one of the Company's boats in 8 minutes ∴ ∴ ∴

A SPECIAL AFTERNOON'S OUTING.—One of the most enjoyable features in the Hongkong programme of sight-seeing is a two hours' trip through the KOWLOON DISTRICT as far as the ancient seat of Chinese Officialdom, the Old Walled City of KAU-LUNG, situated under the Lion's-head Rock at a distance of some four miles, the return being made by crossing the Peninsula and passing through the villages of Mong-kok and Yau-ma-ti ∴ ∴

Interesting impressions of native life with innumerable opportunities for the Camera are to be found throughout the journey ∴ ∴

10 cents—Ferry Fare—each way—10 cents.

Star Ferry, 1938.

Notice to tourists, 1925. The Star Ferry Company provided a cross-harbour ferry every eight minutes. Tourists were assumed to travel first class for ten cents each way. With little to see or do in Tsimshatsui, tourists would cross to Kowloon to catch the train or visit the New Territories.

Star Ferry terminus, Hong Kong Island, 1939.

had a crane on it and it lifted a cradle on to the Praya — you ran your car on to the cradle, which was then roped down. You were taken across to Kowloon, where you were deposited at the sea wall between the Star Ferry and the old Kowloon-Canton railway station. Then you went off. You ordered your lighter for some time in the evening and were picked up and brought back again. On Sundays they ran a half-hourly service and the lighter could take six cars at once."

In spite of the inconvenience of crossing the harbour in such a way, there was enough demand by the late twenties to justify looking into alternative means of getting vehicles across. In January 1927 the small lighters transported 403 cars, 9 lorries, 200 motorbikes and 50 stretcher-cases between the island and Kowloon. The following year it was concluded that a cross-harbour bridge would be impracticable and a tunnel prohibitively expensive, so a vehicular ferry seemed to be the only answer.

The chief means of crossing the harbour for pedestrians was the Star Ferry, established in the late nineteenth century. Commuter traffic was minimal compared to today and the ferry service less efficient. In fact, the Star Ferry Company came in for some bitter criticism: "The company is doing so well out of the public and making such immense profits that they should do something about the service." The journey usually took fifteen minutes, though there were exceptions: on the night of 4 February 1931 a boat left Hong Kong at 1.05 a.m. and reached Kowloon forty minutes later, having gone round in circles in dense fog.

Motor cars appeared in growing numbers in Hong Kong after World War I. The *South China Morning Post* reported in 1922 that "Other things being equal, the man who drives a motor car is likely to live longer than the man who does not; the greatest benefit of the motor car is its gift of fresh air."

In spite of the freedom enjoyed by motorists in those days, there were already problems by 1919. The *South China Morning Post* complained that "during race week, with something like two hundred cars dashing along Des Voeux and Queen's Roads to and from the valley, other traffic had many exceedingly narrow escapes. This was particularly noticeable in Pedder Street, where cars turning abruptly from Queen's Road and Des Voeux Road cut across the stream of pedestrian and rickshaw traffic." Rickshaw coolies were used to taking the centre of the road and turning suddenly without hand signals, so it was not surprising that there were frequent collisions between them and motor cars.

Race-meeting traffic was particularly heavy and by 1930 a new car park had been built to accommodate two hundred cars on Morrison Hill owing to the complaints of wealthy punters unable to find where their chauffeurs were parked. The car park was policed by a European constable, whose job it was to supervise parking and prevent thefts from open-top tourers.

Open tourers were the most popular cars of the day, although wealthier Europeans and Chinese preferred saloons. Open tourers did better on the used-car market, as two or three extra people could be squeezed in during rush hours. The largest market for second-hand cars from Hong Kong was Canton, where they were used for public hire. Business was bad in the car trade in 1930, having been in steady decline since the 1925 strike, after which British cars were overtaken in popularity by the cheaper American models. The *Weekly Press* reported that "The higher quality of workmanship and materials of British cars does not carry any weight with most Chinese buyers, who base their choice on good looks and low initial cost."

Of the 1,412 cars on the road in 1929, the most numerous were the British Austin Sevens (156), with the American Studebakers (137) and Chryslers (130) close runners-up. Italian car manufacturers were represented by Fiat (78) and France by three Bugattis. Rolls-Royces were particularly exclusive in 1929 as only two existed in the colony. The cheaper, flashier Cadillac had twelve models on Hong Kong roads. The Mercedes Benz was not represented at all in Hong Kong.

The proud owner of this late thirties Studebaker is Alec Hutton Potts, master of the Fanling Hunt, seen here with his son Peter.

Harley Davidson, 1931.

Of the 247 taxis on the roads in 1929, the greatest proportion were American makes, with Chryslers predominating. Only thirty-two taxis were British-made. A pioneer of the taxicab in Hong Kong was Mr She Tat-cheong, a former compradore with the Hong Kong and Macau Steamship Company, who launched the Hong Kong and Shanghai Taxicab Company Limited with a fleet of ten Morris cars. In spite of the general depression following the Wall Street crash, he built up his fleet to include the latest American Dodge and Plymouth models. When war came to Hong Kong in December 1941 he placed the whole of his fleet at the service of the colony's defence.

Four hundred and sixty motorcycles made up one third of private motor vehicle traffic in Hong Kong in 1929. The British AJS led the field with 90, followed by the American Harley Davidson with 77, then the British Triumph (64) and BSA (49). Germany was barely in evidence with two BMWs. The most popular machines were in the medium-powered, twin-cylinder, 350-500 c.c. range, having a "much sweeter pulling power on hills and long climbs". Motorcycles with sidecars were not as popular, as they were not much cheaper than small cars and the Chinese sporting youth was "not like the rider at home, who is contented with two wheels rather than four".

By 1929 there were 446 commercial vehicles in Hong Kong and 150 buses. Four years later the Chinese Motor Bus Company and the Kowloon Motor Bus Company were formed to operate buses on the island and Kowloon respectively.

With increased motor traffic there was a growing need for bigger and better roads. Governor Stubbs earned the sobriquet "Road-maker"; Stubbs Road, the road up to the Peak from Magazine Gap, and the Shaukeiwan-Stanley-Repulse Bay-Aberdeen road were all completed during his governorship in the first five years after World War I.

Petrol prices in Hong Kong were comparatively high during the period. A gallon cost eighty-five cents in 1934, compared with fifty-one cents in Shanghai and only forty-five cents in England.

Such was the novelty of the motor car even in 1932 that the *Hongkong Telegraph* ran a weekly "Lucky Motorist" feature, with a photograph of a parked car and an invitation to whoever owned it to collect a free supply of oil from the Texas Company (China) Limited. As late as 1938 the following notice appeared in the classified section of the *South China Morning Post*: "Will the person who removed Austin car 858 on New Year's Eve from near the Star Ferry return it to that vicinity or 'phone 58821."

Eric Himsworth drove a small Standard, which he shared with a friend, David Macdougal, who rose to colonial secretary after the war. "We lived up in Robinson Road and drove to the office down Garden Road, which was about a third of the width it is today. You didn't have to look for a parking place in Central as parking was easy. The main parking places were down the middle of Connaught Road and Pedder Street, but if by chance there wasn't a place, you parked in the middle of Chater Road or round Queen Victoria's statue in Statue Square."

Driving back home to the Mid-levels up narrow Garden Road had its hazards. In 1938 a driver was fined for overtaking three cars and driving up

Castle Peak Road, 1927.

Garden Road on the wrong side. Residents of the Mid-levels and the Peak who wished to avoid such problems (or just did not like driving) would take the Peak Tram. It provided a regular service until five minutes past midnight, but at any time up to three in the morning late-night revellers could "buy a tram". "You could walk into the Peak Tram station on Garden Road," remembers Eric Himsworth, "and say 'I want a tram'. It would cost you two dollars even if you were on your own. They put on a special tram for you, and if one was going up then another had to come down. If you were in a group it cost two dollars for the first four and fifty cents a head for any more." The front section of the tram was reserved for the governor, whose summer retreat, Mountain Lodge, was at the top of the Peak. "If he went up by tram, wishing to avoid going all the way round Wanchai before Magazine Gap Road opened in the early thirties, he had the front seat, which had a sign on it indicating that, if anyone

was in it when the governor appeared, they had to get out."

Another form of transport, which would in the future transform the colony's life more fundamentally than the Peak Tram ever did, was the elevator. Hong Kong's first electric lift had been installed in Queen's Building in 1898, but it was not until fourteen years later that two more lifts appeared, in the Chartered Bank building. In 1934 gearless signal control lifts were installed in the Hong Kong Stock Exchange building. The two-car operation freed lift operators from all duties except pressing buttons and opening and closing doors. By the outbreak of war there were more than two hundred lifts in the colony.

The pace and manner movement in the colony was in effect being transformed by the petrol engine and the electric lift. By 1941 the rickshaw and chair coolies had only a few more years to ply their trade before the motor car drove them off the streets.

Murray Barracks at the junction of Garden Road and Queen's Road Central, 1939.

Aberdeen, 1937.

View of Victoria and the Peak from across the harbour, 1937.

Garden Road, 1939.

View of Garden Road from the Hong Kong Cricket Club, 1939.

The unveiling of the Cenotaph, 11 November 1923.

COME TO HONG KON
THE GATEWAY OF SOUTH CHINA

YOU CANNOT SAY YOU SAW CHINA IF YOU DID NOT SEE THE
HERE IS AN ENTIRELY DIFFERENT ASPECT OF CHINESE LIFE YOU
AFFORD TO MISS. MAKE YOUR HEADQUARTERS IN HONG KONG
THE EAST IN COMFORT. WORLD-FAMED HOTELS WILL CATER
WELL-BEING AND FREQUENT FAST BOAT CONNECTIONS TAKE YOU
TO CANTON AND MACAU.

Overland China Mail, 1935.

The Cenotaph, with Connaught Road in front, 1925.

Dragon boat races in front of the Victoria Rowing Club, 1931.

Pokfulam boulder, 1926. In the worst typhoon since 1898, a three thousand ton boulder fell 250 feet on to the Government Waterworks pumping station, killing four Chinese coolies and injuring four others. Water supplies to the Peak were cut and it cost the government eight thousand dollars to remove the boulder.

The Supreme Court and Statue Square, 1925. The Supreme Court building opened in 1911. Queen Victoria's statue was taken down by the Japanese during the years of occupation. She now rests, without her cupola, in humbler surroundings in King's Park.

Hong Kong at night, 1939.

Bowen Road reservoir from the Ladies' Recreation Club, 1925.

Steamships along the Praya, 1925.

Sedan chair ascending Peel Street, 1925.

Central market, 1939.

Des Voeux Road Central, 1939. Lane, Crawford building, opened in 1926, is on the left.

Pedder Street, 1939.

102

Mid-levels above Kennedy Road, 1937.

The parking area in Statue Square with the Hong Kong Club in the background, 1939.

11
PIRATES AND OPIUM

"I request that immediate steps be taken for the extermination of these pirates, whose immunity for so long a period is a standing disgrace to the Canton government."

Sir Cecil Clementi, 1926

Pirates were common in the seas around Hong Kong before World War II, as they had been ever since the earliest days of the colony. The peasant villages of the south China coastline barely rose above subsistence level, so it was common practice for villages to form pirate bands and prey on the ships and ferries plying to and from Hong Kong. The lawlessness which prevailed in China throughout the warlord era made any kind of co-operation to stamp out piracy between Hong Kong and China almost impossible. Consequently, no journey in Hong Kong waters by any vessel smaller than an ocean liner was safe from the danger of pirate attack. Even ferries to the nearby islands, including Stonecutters in the middle of Hong Kong Harbour, were pirated at one time or another.

Marjorie Angus' brother was an officer on board the Butterfield and Swire ship the *Anking* when it was pirated three days out from Singapore in 1928. "The first thing my brother knew about it was when he heard shooting. He thought at first it was firecrackers going off until the Chinese Number Three fireman came running in: 'Number Three (my brother was third engineer). Plenty trouble topside. Plenty pirate. Plenty killed.' They had shot dead the chief engineer, the chief officer and the doctor and several of the crew. The captain they had shot in the legs. The second officer was OK. They used him to navigate the ship. They kept my brother

for thirty-six hours in the engine room. When they got to Bias Bay they took him ashore as a hostage, but later let him go when he gave them ten dollars. The cabins were looted and everything was in a mess. When they went ashore at Bias Bay one of the pirates had a dinner jacket on, another was wearing a fashionable straw hat. Two or three years later some of the pirates were caught in Shaukeiwan. They had jewellery on them and one was wearing the chief officer's ring with his initials on it."

As Royal Naval patrol boats kept a fairly high profile, it was common for a pirate gang to board a ship as passengers, often in first class. After a day or so at sea the leader would give the signal and the pirates would throw off their feigned respectability, capture the officers, kill those who resisted them, smash the wireless and force the captain to sail the ship at gunpoint to a pirate haven on the south China coast.

Short of searching every single passenger for weapons, it was impossible to detect pirates embarking on board ship. Some were overtly very respectable and it was said of China in the warlord period that a man might be a leading member of the Canton government one day and a pirate the next.

The best-organised gangs had a spy network covering all the ports of South-east Asia and knew exactly what was being shipped where and by whom. The most notorious pirate villages in the

104

The first contingent of the Anti-Piracy Guard for which the police force assumed responsibility in 1930. This group consisted of White Russian guards under the command of a European Sergeant.

Hong Kong area were those in Bias Bay, just north of the colony. A special Hong Kong government commission was set up in 1927 to look into the Bias Bay pirate network. A major problem facing Hong Kong was that Bias Bay lay in Chinese territory and action against the pirates depended on the co-operation of the Chinese authorities. The Hong Kong government was unable to send troops in to Bias Bay, even if it were known that hostages from Hong Kong were being kept there, without the permission of Canton.

Hong Kong's governor, Sir Cecil Clementi, was often frustrated in his attempts to seek the Chinese government's co-operation to stamp out piracy in the area. Following the capture in 1926 of a British subject, a Mr Appleby of the China Telegraph Company, Sir Cecil approached the British consul in Canton. "I request that immediate steps be taken for the extermination of these pirates, whose immunity for so long a period is a standing disgrace to the Canton government." "Put an end to these outrages and so discharge the elementary duties of a civilised administration," thundered the consul-general to the Chinese nationalist government. Mr Appleby was eventually released.

Sir Cecil pursued a similar theme in a speech to the Hong Kong Chamber of Commerce in April 1927. Although the British had offered full naval and military co-operation to the Chinese, "They have rejected these offers of help and they have done nothing whatever themselves, but have been scandalously forgetful of the first duty of any civilised and self-respecting government, namely the suppression of piracy and brigandage and the maintenance of law and order."

In view of the turbulent times, shipping companies spent a lot of money trying to make their vessels pirate-proof. Vessels began to look like floating fortresses, with iron grilling separating the passenger area from the bridge and the engine rooms. The Kwok Hing Shek-ki Ferry Company, after refusing to pay fifty thousand dollars a year in protection money to a local pirate gang, hired two launches manned by armed crews and a fully armed junk to protect its ferries.

Some shipping companies employed Indian guards to keep watch over the ship's bridge. However, evidence brought before the piracy commission in 1927 showed that the guards were often more trouble than they were worth. In its report, the commission stated that the guards had not in fact prevented a single piracy. On board SS

Wing-on, for example, one guard was reported to have dropped his rifle down the stokehold after falling asleep on duty. Another was found asleep in a saloon passengers' chair. One guard was on drugs. Another walked off the ship without notice after an argument with the chief officer about his pay. Yet another guard admitted that he would not know how to fire his gun even if there were a pirate attack. It was hardly surprising that neither shipping companies nor ships' officers had much faith in Indian guards as an answer to the piracy problem.

Piracy was a weekly occurrence in Hong Kong waters in the twenties. In February 1925 pirates became so bold they attacked a Hong Kong and Yaumatei Ferry Company boat plying between Central and Shamshuipo off Stonecutters Island. The ferry was taken towards Macau and the passengers held for ransom, although the boat and all on board were safely rescued by the Royal Navy. For the next four years the company used a second ferry, which was armed, to protect the one carrying passengers after dark.

The most sensational piracy involving a local ferry occurred in 1924 when a Cheung Chau ferry, the *Lee Fat* was captured on its way to Hong Kong. Passengers were taken to a secret hideaway after a forced two-hour march into the mountains on the mainland. One was shot dead trying to escape and seven later died from exposure or maltreatment by the pirates. A bizarre aspect of the kidnapping, which shocked a disbelieving Hong Kong public, was the posting of three of the hostages' ears to relatives in Hong Kong. Ransoms were hastily paid and the hostages were released.

Until the outbreak of the Sino-Japanese War later in the decade, the 1930s saw a gradual decline in the incidence of pirate attacks, as the Chinese authorities were better able to impose law and order in Kwangtung province and the Hong Kong police became more effective in preventing them. In 1930 the military authorities had handed over the job of providing anti-piracy guards for ships leaving Hong Kong to the police, who recruited special guards from north China

and India. Twenty-four White Russians were included in the police anti-piracy guard, and in the first year of the guard's operation none of the ships it protected was attacked.

In 1924 a government committee concluded that up to a quarter of Hong Kong's Chinese population smoked opium and that this state of affairs was unlikely to change unless the government changed its policy of paying commissions to licensed retailers. The government, which derived revenue from the licensed retail shops, failed to act on the committee's advice and eight years were to pass before the government, pressurised further to do something about the widespread smoking of opium in Hong Kong, introduced a law giving the police wider powers to stamp out the illegal divans which proliferated in the colony.

In the mid-thirties there were seventy retail shops selling "government opium" under licence at $14.50 a tael. The shops sold their product at a price which was far too high for the ordinary coolie, so a flourishing black market had developed in which opium could be bought for $3.50 a tael.

Illegal opium divans were usually found in squalid cubicles or bedspaces in tenement buildings. The government estimated that there were between two and three thousand opium divans in Hong Kong, each meeting the needs of up to forty smokers a day. Police raids were frequent after the Opium Ordinance was passed in 1932 but did little to solve the problem, as many policemen used the raids as an opportunity to extort money from divan organisers. Smokers were rarely arrested as there was no room for them in Hong Kong's overcrowded gaols.

Attempts to control the supply of black-market opium coming into Hong Kong were hampered by the fact that unrestricted entry into the colony made it impossible to exercise proper controls over the daily ebb and flow of people crossing the border by foot, train, steamer, junk or sampan. The long, indented coastline made it easy for a junk to land a consignment of opium undetected, and the patrolling vessels in Hong Kong waters were powerless against sampan crews

Superstructure of a vessel pirated in Hong Kong waters, 1925. In spite of iron grilles which turned vessels into floating fortresses, pirate gangs were a constant menace to ships plying the South China Sea between the wars. In the case of this ship, the pirates seized the officers at gun-point, sailed the ship to their haven in Bias Bay and set the upper decks on fire after seizing cargo and passengers' effects.

who would throw contraband overboard if they were spotted. Fixed to floats made to sink for a while before rising to the surface, the contraband could be picked up after the patrolling vessel had gone. Hong Kong's customs officers were often in collusion with the smugglers, as were many Kwangtung officials.

Widespread poverty in south China and Hong Kong provided an army of agents and drug runners only too eager to make an income from a habit which had long been customary among the Chinese of both societies. The 1924 committee had stated that opium smoking in China probably had the same popular support as betting had in England and that stopping its flow into Hong Kong was as impossible a task as "preventing the use in Manchester of an article in common use in England". The government put the blame for opium addiction not on its own lack of determination to stamp it out but on the attitude of the Chinese in Hong Kong whose apathy and indifference to helping police anti-narcotic investigations were "deplorable".

The authorities also took the view that they were no match for the ingenuity of the professional Chinese smuggler. Hong Kong's role as an entrepot and its key position on the world's steamship routes made the colony the centre of a highly organised international traffic in drugs. The cost of fighting this, according to the government, imposed "all too severe a drain on the local domestic resources". On the other hand, the government was happy to report in 1939 that "the sales of government opium increased considerably during the year . . . "

Meanwhile, coolie addicts suffered the effects of their addiction in ruined health and malnutrition. Some might end up in hospital (in 1935 there were 478 opium cases treated in the Tung Wah Eastern Hospital and 37 in the Government Civil Hospital), while others were left to die in the streets. Europeans, who were not averse to an occasional smoke at Chinese dinners or while doing business with a Chinese firm, would only occasionally see what happened to the coolie addict. Marjorie Angus would sometimes walk past an opium divan and see addicts "lying as if they were dead, on shelves. They were skeletal as they didn't eat. Suddenly they would jump up like new people, transformed for a few hours until they collapsed and needed another smoke. Lifelessness to great energy, until they got slower and slower . . . "

12

THE LINE

"Many Hong Kong flappers favour biblical gowns these days. Sort of low and behold!"

Hongkong Telegraph, *1932*

"The climate of Hong Kong, being semi-tropical, produces unnatural fecundity. This is coupled with the fact that the men here, coming mainly from abroad, are somewhat irresponsible, the more so if they are young and single."

Letter to the Hongkong Telegraph, *1932*

It was commonly believed between the wars that European men outnumbered women in Hong Kong by ten to one, a belief based not so much on hard statistics as on the fact that there seemed to be so many more men around than women. Employment contracts for most major firms stipulated that men were not allowed to marry until they were in their late twenties at least, and the same applied to the services. Even so, permission for marriage had to be sought from the firm.

The choice a wife faced of either leaving the husband to be with the children in England or leaving the children to be with the husband in Hong Kong provided a great dilemma for many couples, though for some it was doubtless an easy choice. In the days when divorce and separation were socially unacceptable, to live apart on these terms provided a viable alternative. But for all the husbands who were glad to be rid of their wives, and vice versa, there were those who keenly felt the pain of separation.

Among the Chinese community of Hong Kong, men outnumbered women for different reasons. Most Chinese were of the coolie class, the men having left their families in Kwangtung to live in boarding houses, although this pattern began to change by the early thirties, which saw more families coming in.

For a young woman like Marjorie Angus, being a single girl in Hong Kong was "damned good" as there was a high premium on unmarried women, the more so if they were attractive and susceptible to male charms. Many single girls came out to Hong Kong in the so-called "fishing fleet" in the hope of catching an eligible bachelor from one of the big firms or, better still, the services. For Peggy Beard, servicemen were at an advantage as they were freer in the daytime than civilians. She met her husband-to-be, Kenneth, when he came out to Hong Kong in 1927 with the Fleet Air Arm on his way to protect British interests at Shanghai as part of the Shanghai Defence Force. As it turned out, the "Sha-force" stayed at Kai Tak with nothing to do but go out on dawn patrol looking for pirates in Bias and Mirs Bays. Peggy and her friends served tea and coffee to the men off duty, and it was in these circumstances that her romance with Kenneth blossomed. He would fly his seaplane out to the family bungalow in Shek-O to see her, and on 18 December 1928 they were married in St John's Cathedral.

For outgoing single girls life could be a constant round of launch and beach picnics, tea dances, balls, bridge and mah-jong sessions and evenings spent listening to regimental bands under a starry sky. Few single girls came out specifically to work as there were limited career opportunities for women in Hong Kong, although some found employment as governesses, private nurses or as secretaries in banks or commercial houses. Marjorie Angus worked as an assistant in the central curio shop, the Jade Tree; Peggy Beard's four bridesmaids all had jobs as secretaries.

Most single girls lived with their parents. For those without families, accommodation was available at the Helena May Institute in Garden Road, the so-called "virgins' retreat", where a strict maternal code was enforced. Marjorie Angus says that Lady Clementi read all new books bought for the Helena May library. "Any reference to a kiss or a cuddle and the book was removed." One such book was *Blue Lagoon*; its withdrawal from the library instantly made it a best-seller.

Because of the poor ratio of men to women, the world's oldest profession flourished in Hong Kong. Legalised brothels regularly had the services of a health inspector until a change of heart caused the government to close them down in 1932. Marjorie Angus holds Lady Clementi responsible, while others maintained that the closure was the result of pressure from the League of Nations and Britain's first woman member of Parliament, Lady Astor. Eric Himsworth, on the other hand, is convinced that the clamp-down was due to the efforts of a triumvirate of powerful wives: Mrs Wolfe, married to the inspector-general of police, Mrs Tratman, married to the secretary of Chinese affairs, and Lady Southorn, the wife of the Colonial Secretary. Like many others at the time, Eric Himsworth believed that the closure of legalised brothels was a pity as it drove prostitutes underground and denied them and their clients the benefits of regular health inspection. As a result, he remembers that venereal disease was reported to have spread so much among troops stationed in Hong Kong that the colony had the highest incidence of any British station overseas. The Reverend Sandbach of the Methodist Church, which ran the Soldiers' and Sailors' Home in Wanchai, was so alarmed at

Soldiers' and Sailors' Home, Wanchai, 1939.

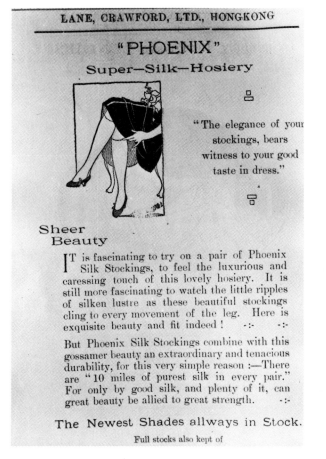

Lane, Crawford catalogue, 1926. Bare legs in the street or on the golf course or tennis court were unthinkable for European women in the twenties. No woman would leave the house without her silk stockings on, whatever the weather, and habitually wore stockings even at home.

Hongkong Telegraph, 1930. By the early thirties the short hemlines of the flapper era were beginning to drop and, for the bolder Hong Kong woman, giving way to the trouser suit.

the growing number of prostitutes in the area that he personally wrote to the governor requesting the re-opening of legalised brothels.

Other Hong Kong clergymen were less sympathetic to women in Hong Kong. In an outspoken sermon given at the nine o'clock mass at Rosary Church in Kowloon in June 1934, Reverend Father H. De Angelis soundly condemned women and what they were: "For a pair of short pants or for a high split skirt she is ready to fall on her knees before the infernal serpent, of whom she is the right hand in the work of dissolution and further destruction . . . A woman who dresses herself in the style that appeals to the baser male instincts can do much mischief and is more powerful than a fully equipped army."

The issue of legalised brothels created a wave of public indignation. "Homo" wrote to the *Hongkong Telegraph* in March 1932 and complained bitterly that their closure had lowered the supply

South China Morning Post, *1939.*

Lane, Crawford catalogue, mid-twenties.

of women who "have at least been playing the sex game honestly". He went on to say that "Hong Kong's greatest peril today lies in the fact that there is a chronic shortage of the female sex . . . The female is ridiculously overvalued out here and from the moment of her arrival . . . sets out to take the fullest possible advantage of it. In Hong Kong, salaries are dissipated wantonly, careers wrecked, lives embittered and strong men are on their knees craving for displays in the nude . . . "

Hong Kong's best-known street for bordellos was Lyndhurst Terrace off Hollywood Road, known affectionately by patrons as "the Line". Here the prostitutes were French, English, American or Australian, with names like Fifi, Nanette, Sarah Bernhardt or Mae West, and their

rooms were exotically furnished in heavy velvet and lace. The queen of "the Line" was Ethel Morrison, who held a place in Hong Kong society similar to the great courtesans of London and Paris. Marjorie Angus remembers her as "a most beautiful woman, with a chest like snow and red hair, who loaned money to young men who got into trouble. She looked about thirty even when she was seventy. The second officer on my husband's ship was so infatuated with one of her girls that he blew his brains out."

According to Austin Coates, Ethel Morrison was Russian, blonde and buxom, and acquired her English surname from the first lover she had really liked, who told her he lived in Morrison Hill. Not knowing much English at the time, the name intrigued her and she adopted it. At Happy

Valley race meetings she moved about graciously, looking all the ladies straight in the face and never even glancing at the men.

Malcolm Swan had her pointed out to him once in whispers, but was then too young to know what she did. All he remembers from the occasion was that she had "a face as hard as granite". He was later told that she had come to Hong Kong in 1906 and then went to Europe to get married, but her fiancé had taken all her savings and abandoned her. It was said at the time that a bachelor on leave met her in Europe and, hearing she needed help, organised a whip-round among his friends in Hong Kong to pay her fare back.

In those days it was customary to hand over a chit for goods or services rendered, and then pay up at the end of the month. Ethel Morrison got bad debtors to pay up in her own special way. Austin Coates has said that "on more than one occasion she paraded into Hong Kong Electric in a wave of French perfume, wafted herself with conviction into the chairman's office and did not leave until the miscreant debtor, whoever it was, was found and had paid up".

Attendance at St John's Cathedral provided no escape from accountability to Ethel, who was reported to have dealt with bad debts by endorsing "Line" chits over the bishop and dropping them into the collection plate. When she died, a memorial service was held for her at the cathedral, for she had given a good deal of money to charity. The service was well attended by local VIPs who made no bones about having admired — if not visited — her.

Some prominent members of Hong Kong's establishment were very closely tied to the ladies of Lyndhurst Terrace. The boss of the accounting firm of Deacon left a major part of his will to one "Ethel Morrissey" of Lyndhurst Terrace. When he died in 1920 after a respectable retirement at Weymouth, the money found its way back to "the Line". Sir Paul Catchik Chater, one of Hong Kong's leading benefactors, had at the age of sixty-four married an attractive Scandinavian brunette less than half his age. Their marriage in 1910 took the new Lady Chater out of Lyndhurst Terrace for good. She nevertheless remained persona non grata at Government House.

Eric Himsworth, who claims never to have patronised "the Line" himself, knew many who did. Having enjoyed the company of the ladies for the night, his friends would, after a shave, a wash and brush up, leave "the Line" in the morning and walk or take a chair down to the office to attend to the day's business.

Eric Himsworth's first job when he came to Hong Kong in 1929 was as deputy registrar of the Supreme Court, where he sat in temporarily for Dickie Melbourne, a bachelor in his sixties who had gone on leave. "Dickie drove an Armstrong Siddely, the number plate of which was 18, which he had removed from number 18 Lyndhurst Terrace. When he retired he gave the car to the chief justice, Sir Joseph Kemp, who drove it around Hong Kong proudly bearing the number plate. Ethel Morrison herself drove around Hong Kong with a driver, never recognising anyone publicly. But she never passed Dickie Melbourne in the street without Dickie raising his hat. A hundred per cent gentleman."

If a bachelor wanted someone a little cheaper than the girls of "the Line" he went down Queen's Road to the Chinese boarding houses of the West Point area. "You were given a cubicle furnished with a wooden bed, and you asked the boy to fetch you a girl if you didn't already have one. You had to sign your name on a list, which was sent up to Central Police station. Among the columns of Chinese names there invariably appeared Sir William and Lady Peel, or whoever was governor at the time."

When "the Line" closed down, the European prostitutes moved to premises in Happy Valley, and advertisements began to appear in the classified sections of the newspapers for "a lost pussycat" or "a nice little puppy dog for sale". Old hands knew what they would find there. When Ethel Morrison died, her place in Happy Valley was taken over by one of her American girls, who kept it going until the Japanese attack in 1941.

Sin-yu, a sing-song girl of Western district, 1936. Western district was the major area for Chinese entertainment, with restaurants, tea houses, mah-jong parlours and brothels. Sin-yu worked in the leading Western restaurants Kan Ling, President and Kwangchou. She was paid one dollar for sitting down with a man for a while and singing songs from Chinese opera. The names of girls were included on the menu and male customers wrote down the name of the girl they were interested in on a piece of paper. Sin-yu later became the concubine of a customer who enjoyed her singing.

The girls of Wanchai were often the only source of female company for the ordinary British soldier stationed in Hong Kong. Bob Yates, who came out to Hong Kong as a gunner on coastal defence duties with the Royal Artillery in 1938, recalls the great gulf which existed between the British Tommy and European women at that time. "There was no point in trying to ask out English girls as they wouldn't even look at you. We soldiers and the Chinese prostitutes had a lot in common. They were outcasts from their society and we were outcasts from ours."

Soldiers like Bob Yates spent a lot of their free time in Wanchai. "Places like the China Fleet Club, the Soldiers' and Sailors' Home, the Luk Kwok Hotel, if you were looking for a better-class prostitute and paid more, Nagasaki Joe's or the Black Dog, which was run by an American ex-petty officer, were the best places to find a girl . . . The Chinese girls in Wanchai were wonderful and you went with them for what was

"Way down in Wanchai there is a place of fame.
There stands a street, and Lockhart is its name.
Slant-eyed Chinese maidens all around I see
Calling out 'Artillery man, abide with me!'

Then on a Friday when I draws my pay,
Straight down to Wanchai I quickly make my way.
Don't find it difficult, so many girls I see,
To find a special one to abide with me.

Two or three days later I looks at
my Hampton Wick
I says to myself, says I, I think you'd better go sick.
Now that I'm better, no more girls for me.
Instead I'll sing in the Cheerio Club
'Abide with me'."

called 'a short time', which cost you two dollars on pay day or one dollar at weekends. They paraded up and down outside the Soldiers' and Sailors' Home and the China Fleet Club in their cheongsams, split up to the thigh, with their hair done in European fashion."

The line of conversation when meeting a girl followed a familiar pattern. " 'Where you go, Georgie?' They called everybody 'Georgie' until they got to know you." Bob Yates tells the story about a new recruit who had come out from Stanley and gone down to Wanchai on his first Saturday night in Hong Kong. Lying in the next morning, his mates in the barrack room said: " 'What you do last night?' and this kid says, 'Went to Wanchai.' 'How d'you get on?' 'Wonderful,' he says. 'Ain't those girls wonderful?' 'How d'you mean wonderful?' 'D'you know?' he says. 'Never been there before. One of them comes up and says, Hallo Georgie! Where you go? How did she know my name was Georgie?' "

Like a number of soldiers, Bob Yates maintained a girl in her cubicle apartment in Western district. In barrack-room language the girls were called "down homers" or, more colloquially, "dahnomers". " 'Where you going, Bill?' 'I'm going dahn 'ome.' But it was far from being a home because all it was was a place in one of those Chinese tenement buildings. A large room was divided up into cubicles by partitions which were about seven feet high and nine feet by twelve feet at the most. The girl would rent one of these and you'd give her five dollars a week, which was six shillings and three pence, and she would do wonders with that. She'd sooner have that than go picking up blokes. She'd be there whenever you went down and if you were to say, 'I'll be down tomorrow and then I'm going out,' she'd say, 'What you put on?' 'I'll put my khakis on,' and you went down there and your buttons were cleaned for you and your cap badge polished and you'd just get dressed and go out and she never said, 'Can I come with you?'

"I had a 'dahnomer', a wonderful little girl. She came from Macau and had a cubicle in Kennedy Town. When I started going with her she had this

Chinese girls, 1939. These photographs found their way into the album of Gunner Bob Yates. A girl such as these might well become a soldier's "dahnomer".

little pigtail. I got into trouble saying that in Hong Kong. A Chinese bloke told me: 'We don't use that word, pigtail. Queue, we call it. We're not pigs.'

"Anyway, this girl wore a coolie dress, black jacket and trousers. She was attractive to me like that. I liked the cheongsam — it was attractive — and the European hairstyle, but somehow the natural way was better on her. One night I went 'down home' and she had a cheongsam on and her hair was shingled. She was as proud as punch. I took one look and started playing hell with her, and she started crying. 'You no like?' And I said, 'No, it's terrible! Where's your pigtail?' She pulled out a box from under the bed and there it was. She had put red tape at the top and at the bottom. I said to her, 'Can I have it?', and she said, 'What for you want?' 'I just want to keep.' 'All right, you keep. But when you no want, you no burn, you no put in fire. You put fire — me die.' Hell, this was just a Chinese superstition. She believed that if her hair was burnt she would die.

'No,' I said, 'I won't burn it.' 'You no want, you put in ground. Bury it, you see.'

"Well, I fully intended to do this. In June 1941 we were told 'Stand by for troopship', so I said to her, 'I'm going back to England. I'll have to pack you in.' They were quite used to this sort of thing, though she wasn't because no one had ever kept her before. Anyway, the girls sort of accepted that one day you'd go back to England.

"I never did get on that troop ship. The war came and I took that pigtail to the prison camp in Shamshuipo. When I was transferred to Japan I took it with me. When the Japanese searched my kit, as they did every so often, they would say of the pigtail, 'Wai-fu?' and I'd say, 'Wai-fu.'

"And do you know, I had that pigtail until the day they dropped the atom bomb on Hiroshima. That day our camp was bombed and shelled by an American task force. The pigtail was in my kit and the whole lot was burnt. I'm not superstitious, but I often wondered what did happen to her."

13

CHINESE WOMEN

"The school was founded to give the girls of the East the very best of the culture of both East and West, and thus to promote goodwill and understanding between nation and nation."

Principal's Speech Day address,
St Stephen's College, 1929

Chinese girls growing up in Hong Kong in the twenties and thirties lived in difficult times. The aim of St Stephen's College to give them the best of East and of West created in many a cultural identity crisis which drew them away from families whose values and attitudes they began to question. One of Sir Robert Ho-tung's daughters, Irene Cheng, who gained degrees from Hong Kong, Columbia and London between the wars, exemplified the new breed of wealthy Chinese women who suffered emotional strain caused by a traditional Chinese upbringing combined with a Western education.

"We grew up in a semi-feudalistic society where normally a family such as ours stayed put in one place, in fact seldom left the family home and lived very much for one another. Parental authority reigned supreme and one's horizon was pretty much limited to the clan. On the other hand, we had to adapt to different ideas and ideals, where members of a family may have had to be separated, often for long periods of time and where the goal, at its most ideal, is to serve society rather than familial or personal ends. We have also had to learn to think for ourselves."

Educational opportunities for Chinese girls expanded greatly between the wars and so opened up the possibility of higher social position and jobs in business and the professions. Until the early twenties, upper-class Chinese women

appeared only rarely in public with their husbands, and then usually only at charity bazaars. Poor Chinese girls were kept at home or lived with the families of husbands-to-be to whom they were betrothed at a very early age. Alternatively, they became concubines or were sold to better-off families as mui-tsai. Again, until the early twenties, arranged marriages were the norm in traditional Chinese families, who thought of marriage as an alliance between families rather than as a personal bond between individuals. Professional matchmakers were often employed to find suitable candidates for marriage. They would visit families in which there were young and suitable girls, ask for the date and hour of their birth and then try to interest the parents of unmarried boys in the proposed match. Details of the date and hour of birth were regarded as highly significant as it was believed that astrological methods could foretell if the two young people would be suitable for each other. If all went well, the young man would be told by his parents of the proposed betrothal and allowed to see the girl, but only from a distance. The girl had no such opportunity. Only by the late twenties were the betrothed pair given the chance to actually meet each other.

Concubinage was common throughout the household servants. The fact that money changed hands and the girls became the property of their period. Women from poorer families, or mui-tsai who had grown up in better-off homes, considered themselves very lucky if they were chosen as a concubine by a wealthy man. The status of a concubine was half-way between a full member of the family and a respected servant, so daughters of wealthy or highly respected families would rarely consent to concubinage. Instead, they could become an "equal wife", or *p'ing ts'ai*, like Irene Cheng's mother, Lady Clara Ho-tung. Sir Robert Ho-tung had been married for fourteen years but his wife, Lady Margaret, had borne him no children. She herself arranged the marriage between Sir Robert and Lady Clara. As "equal wife" there was a proper marriage ceremony in 1895. Lady Clara went on to produce eight girls and three boys, who were taught to call her "Mamma" as opposed to "Mother", the name they used for their father's first wife. Lady Clara called Lady Margaret "Elder Cousin" and she in turn called Lady Clara "Younger Cousin", although friends and acquaintances distinguished the two by the terms "Stouter Madam" and "Slimmer Madam".

Until the early twenties Chinese women in Hong Kong had little protection under the law. A married woman had no rights to property nor could she sue for divorce, because the outdated marriage laws of the Ch'ing dynasty were still in force in Hong Kong, even though the dynasty itself had been legally abolished by the Chinese Revolution of 1911. The nationalist China civil code of 1930 gave equal inheritance rights to sons and daughters, but the Hong Kong government, not wishing to interfere with traditional Chinese customs, maintained the Ch'ing law. The law was particularly hard on women in the New Territories, who were forbidden to inherit land or the implements to farm it.

Moreover, disputes and grievances of women in polygamous marriages (both principal wives and concubines) could not be heard in Hong Kong's courts, which had jurisdiction only over monogamous marriages. In the Ch'ing marriage code a man could "oust his wife for bearing him no son, for . . . laziness, for failure to serve the parents-in-law, for loquacity, which included mischief-making, quarrelsome conduct, larceny, jealousy or incurable disease".

It was this kind of arrangement which the increasing educational opportunities for Chinese girls in Hong Kong between the wars served, overtly or otherwise, to undermine. Schools like St Stephen's College run by Christian organisations promoted, if only indirectly, the dignity and equality of women, although old traditions died hard.

In government schools there was a gradual change to a more Westernised education. The most important, the Belilios Public School, moved in the twenties from a curriculum which prepared girls solely for the role of housewife, with its emphasis on needlework and domestic science, to one which included mathematics, science and art. Sports and community work were encouraged for the first time.

In 1921, ten years after its founding, Hong Kong University admitted its first female students but not without a fight. Many people had taken the view, as Vice Chancellor Hornell later put it, that "this mixing up of the sexes is entirely opposed to Chinese ideas and that the women students will be a perpetual distraction to the men".

However, Hornell himself was proud of the fact that women had been admitted. In 1925 he observed that "women students take their share in nearly all spheres of activity — they play hockey, tennis and attend all social and other functions. At least one woman is at the moment an obvious power for good, not only among the women students but among the men also."

Irene Cheng was one of the first three women undergraduates admitted to the university. Her mother, Lady Clara Ho-tung, had never held the traditional Chinese view that it was virtuous for a woman to be uneducated, but believed that her children should get the best possible Western education and at the same time keep alive their Chinese heritage. Although raised in a traditional atmosphere of female subservience, Lady Clara herself became highly involved in Hong Kong

South China Morning Post, 1939. As a local guide book commented, "Discarded with her old-fashioned dress are the old-fashioned restrictions, and the present-day Chinese Miss would laugh at the idea of an amah chaperone accompanying her on her daily round of shopping, tea dancing and picture-going with her boyfriends."

public life. Motivated by her Buddhist beliefs, her interests included medical, social and educational work. In 1930 she set up the Po Kok Free Schools for poor children in Macau and Hong Kong after a visit to Dr Barnardo's homes in England, and in 1935 established a Buddhist temple, Tung Lin Kok Yuen, which incorporated the Po Kok School and Po Kok Buddhist Seminary. She built a dogs' home, being a committee member of the Hong Kong Society for the Protection of Animals. She was particularly interested in medical work and, after the outbreak of the Sino-Japanese War, helped raise funds and organise relief for China as vice-president of the Hong Kong Chinese Women's Relief Association, of which Sun Yat-sen's widow was president.

The Relief Association, together with the Hong Kong Chinese Women's Club, founded in 1938 with the similar aim of providing relief for China during the war against Japan, did much to raise the level of consciousness among Chinese women in Hong Kong, albeit women from the upper classes. More universal in its appeal to all classes of women and generally considered to be at the vanguard of the women's movement in Hong Kong was the YWCA, established in the colony in 1920. Originally set up to promote Christianity and charity work and to provide accommodation for single female travellers passing through Hong Kong to China, it later developed educational and recreational activities for illiterates, amahs, housewives and businesswomen. The aim of its short-lived monthly magazine, *The Voices of Women in Hong Kong*, the colony's first women's magazine, was "to serve as the only means of expression for Hong Kong women, concerning legal status, marriage, educational opportunities, equal pay and welfare".

The YWCA had to tread carefully. In 1931 a campsite founded at Tsuen Wan for Chinese girls met with opposition from parents shocked at the thought of their daughters sleeping out away from home, and the general strike and boycott of 1925-26 made the government particularly wary of any organisation with political overtones. The YWCA did not advance the legal status of women, but its charitable work, in the absence of a social welfare department in government, did much to raise the expectations and opportunities for Chinese women in Hong Kong.

It was, therefore, not surprising that women in the organisation took the lead in fighting what many considered to be the most degrading institution affecting women in Hong Kong, the mui-tsai system.

14

MUI-TSAI

"Slavery exists in the British Crown colony of Hong Kong today under the mui-tsai and kindred systems. No centenary celebrations of the abolition of slavery in British possessions, however numerous, will alter the fact."

Commander H.L. Haslewood, RN, at the British Commonwealth League Annual Conference, 1934

The controversial issue of child slavery in Hong Kong highlighted the division between the liberal ideas of the West and the traditions and culture of old China. The issue revolved around the mui-tsai system, in which poor Chinese girls were sold by their families to work as unpaid servants in the households of those who could afford to buy them. It was a very old Chinese practice which, in the humanitarian atmosphere following the "war to end all wars", came under considerable attack during the twenties and thirties by those holding liberal Western opinions. The issue was discussed in detail at the newly established League of Nations in Geneva and on the floor of the British House of Commons. Such was the pressure on the British government to end what seemed to be a blight on the good name of the British empire that the secretary of state for the colonies, Winston Churchill, cabled Hong Kong's governor, Sir Reginald Stubbs, in 1922 ordering him to put an end to female child slavery in the colony.

In Hong Kong itself the issue not only caused a split between liberal Westerners and traditional Chinese, but also created fissures within the Chinese community itself. The Society for the Protection of Mui-tsai represented the conservative view that the system should be maintained

and the girls protected, while the more radical Anti-Mui-tsai Society aimed at the total abolition of the mui-tsai system. The former consisted of many prominent Chinese businessmen who no doubt owned mui-tsai themselves and saw the merits of such long-established Chinese customs. The latter were mainly Chinese Christians who considered the system to be immoral and anti-Christian.

A major problem in the discussion of the rights and wrongs of the mui-tsai system lay in the question of definition. To the Westerner, mui-tsai meant "girl slave", but it was never quite as simple as that. *Mui* in Cantonese means "younger sister" and *tsai* means "little", "boy" or "son". Mui-tsai, therefore, could be a term of endearment and was commonly used for any young girl. However, the words took on different connotations according to who was using them and to whom they were addressed. A British woman looking into the question offended a Hong Kong street urchin in 1936 when she asked the little girl if she were a mui-tsai. In the words of the woman's interpreter, the girl's reply was "May you go away and die."

As generally understood, the mui-tsai system involved the buying and selling of young girls as masters was enough to equate the system with slavery in the eyes of many. On the other hand, it was traditional Chinese practice to make money transactions to seal a number of social agreements – betrothal, marriage, concubinage or mui-tsai.

Many girls were sold in Hong Kong and China for a limited period only. They served as pledge for a loan to settle gambling debts, buy opium or, in the rural New Territories, to buy farm stock and could be redeemed by their parents if and when the loan were paid off.

Undoubtedly the system lent itself to exploitation. The girls were young and uneducated, had no rights or liberties and could be made to work for as many hours as their owners decided with little or no pay. Many mui-tsai ended up as prostitutes. Eighteen-year old Fung Mui told the following story to Hong Kong's secretary for Chinese affairs: "I have been acting as a prostitute since I was deflowered at Canton when I was sixteen. My parents died and I was brought up by a man and his wife in Fat Shan. The man died and the widow treated me well, but as she was hard up she consulted me about selling me. I consented to being sold, but at first did not know that I was to be sold into a brothel in Canton. I was thirteen at the time and was taken to a house occupied by the family of a brothel keeper. My "pocket mother" asked me to see what a pleasant life these prostitutes were leading. I saw all the prostitutes wore beautiful clothes and had gold bangles and finger rings on. I then turned my mind to be brought up as a prostitute. I was then taught to sing and can now sing over ten songs. At fifteen I was resold to one of the brothel boats; it was on the sixteenth day of the first moon of my sixteenth year that my virginity was taken away."

The opponents of the mui-tsai system cited similar examples, comparing it to black slavery in America and serfdom in tsarist Russia. Why, they argued, should the British colony of Hong Kong perpetuate a system which America and Russia had abolished years ago? The system allowed young girls to be ill-treated, neglected, seduced or forced into prostitution. They could be made to do anything which their owners demanded of them. Moreover, the system encouraged parents to part with their children in order to enjoy a better life, gamble or smoke opium.

In its 1921 manifesto the Anti-Mui-tsai Society summed up the case for abolition. The system contravened humanitarian principles as it allowed human beings to be treated as commercial property; it was immoral, as it allowed girls to be exploited sexually or tortured physically by their masters; it harmed the international prestige of the Chinese race; it ran against the evolutionary progress of society in its denial of equal rights; and it was essentially unbiblical.

The Anti-Mui-tsai Society was predominantly Christian in its membership and was actively supported by the churches in Hong Kong. However, many of the Chinese élite in Hong Kong considered abolitionist arguments an affront to traditional Chinese culture. A leader of opinion among the traditionalists, Mr Chow Shou-son, articulated the views of the Society for the Protection of Mui-tsai when he spoke out against immediate abolition in 1923. "Those in favour of the bill have undoubtedly been activated by generous motives and lofty ideals, but I am afraid their burning zeal has not permitted them to study the problem with that calmness and impartiality which the importance of the subject demands. I do not keep, and have never kept, any mui-tsai, but this does not blind me to the unwisdom of trying to sweep away in a day the custom with its good points."

The protectionists argued that the mui-tsai system was basically a Chinese tradition and that mui-tsai were different from girls brought up for prostitution. They claimed that mui-tsai were seldom exploited sexually by their masters and that if they subsequently became concubines it was done with the approval of the mistress of the house. They took the view that the system was in fact an act of charity as the mui-tsai could live a better life in their master's household and the system helped poor families by rewarding them financially and saving them from having to drown their surplus baby daughters.

Selling a daughter for money was as common in poverty-stricken areas of China as were famines, floods, droughts, pestilence and banditry. In the absence of poor laws or a system of social welfare, the sale of a daughter in China was often the only means of preserving a girl's life. During hard times it was accepted as being normal and natural for an individual to be sacrificed for the sake of the family.

Mr Harry Ching, the editor of the *South China Morning Post*, estimated in 1937 that every second Chinese household kept at least one mui-tsai. Many were bought by childless couples who wanted a daughter, by widows or spinsters seeking a companion, by elderly women whose own daughters had grown up or by concubines whose daughters were regarded as children of the first wife. Poor Chinese families in Hong Kong kept a mui-tsai to look after the children when the wife went out to work.

Mr Chow Shou-son may have denied ever having kept mui-tsai, but most prominent Chinese and Eurasian families did keep them. Sir Robert and Lady Clara Ho-tung each had mui-tsai of their own. Their daughter, Irene Cheng, felt that the system was much misunderstood and misinterpreted by Westerners because in her parents' households mui-tsai were well treated and often educated. She recognised that, whereas it was possible for men to escape the economic hardships of south China by finding work in Hong Kong or abroad, voluntary emigration for women was out of the question.

Even the League of Nations officially recognised merits in the system, concluding that a mui-tsai was often in a better position than a paid household servant. Far from leading to prostitution, it was felt by some that the true mui-tsai system was a protection against it. Most mui-tsai eventually married and could look upon the home and family of their former masters as their own.

Young boys could also be given away or sold for adoption. However, boys were only sold as a last resort, because they carried on the ancestral line. Nevertheless, Hong Kong's governor, Sir Cecil Clementi, told of famine-stricken parents in the Pearl estuary begging passengers from Hong Kong to accept children – boys as well as girls – who would otherwise starve. The chairman of Hong Kong's 1935 Mui-tsai Committee related an incident that had happened when he was stationed in Penang. His own three year old son had no one to play with, so the family's Cantonese amah suggested he buy a Chinese boy as a playmate for his son. The amah assured him that sturdy, healthy boys cost no more than fifty or sixty dollars and there were plenty on offer.

Although opposition to the buying and selling of Chinese children in Hong Kong had begun in the late nineteenth century, it was not until after World War I that it became strident. This was largely due to the zeal and determination of a British couple, Lieutenant-Commander H.L. Haslewood and his wife, who had come out to Hong Kong in 1919 when Haslewood was appointed superintendent of the naval chart depot. They were shocked at the existence of slave girls and, frustrated in their attempts to rouse public opinion in the colony against the mui-tsai system, resolved to return to England to raise the matter there. Fired by a deep sense of mission, they sailed back to Britain in the early 1920s and stunned both Parliament and the nation with their revelation that child slavery continued to exist in a British colony.

As a result the British government put pressure on the Hong Kong government to abolish the mui-tsai system. Winston Churchill cabled Governor Stubbs in February 1922 to effect abolition within a year. Churchill was adamant. "It is impossible for me to defend the existence of such an institution in a British colony if I am unable to state that no slightest element of compulsory employment is involved, this becoming the essence of slavery."

Unlike Churchill, the governor had first-hand knowledge of the strength of traditional Chinese feeling. The Society for the Protection of Mui-tsai had just been formed (1921), and the bill for abolition which Churchill demanded encountered strong opposition from the Chinese representatives of the Legislative Council. Stubbs was reluctant to press the matter. "From a social point of view Hong Kong cannot be separated from China and it would be disastrous for the government to act in direct opposition to overwhelming public opinion." The Hong Kong government knew that to alienate powerful Chinese mercantile interests was bad business, so a compromise was reached with the Female Service Ordinance of 1923, which fell short of abolition but stated that no new mui-tsai were to be engaged and existing ones were to be registered.

Arguments generated between 1920-22 surfaced again in the wake of Stubb's compromise. The Anti-Mui-tsai Society began a massive propaganda campaign, with essay competitions, publicity songs, pamphlets and speeches for emancipation at church meetings and schools. The abolitionists won over many labour unions, who supported their opposition to the powerful Chinese business interests. The society won the support of the foreign community, largely through the efforts of its English secretary, C.G. Anderson, who wrote regularly to the English-language newspapers.

The general strike of 1925 and the year-long boycott of Hong Kong's trade by Canton channelled Hong Kong's energies in different directions, but the mui-tsai question came into focus once again in 1927 when the nationalist Chinese government ended slavery and the mui-tsai system throughout the mainland. The Anti-Mui-tsai Society was mobilised into renewed activity that year, after an article appeared in the Hong Kong Chinese newspaper, *Wa Tsing Yat Po*, claiming that the sale of children in Hong Kong had shot up following the new law in China. Public opinion was inflamed again when a Mr M.J.H. Harris of the Anti-Slavery and Aborigines Protection Society in Britain wrote a letter to the *Manchester Guardian* stating that the mui-tsai system was still in operation and that the number of mui-tsai in Hong Kong was increasing.

The League of Nations, meanwhile, faced the issue once again and its 1931 Report of the Committee of Experts on Slavery focused international attention on the mui-tsai system.

The Hong Kong government was still loathe to push through total abolition, but in 1929 amended the 1923 ordinance to tighten up the registration of all mui-tsai in order to ensure their protection. Registration was all very well in theory, but difficult to carry out in practice. With the ebb and flow of Chinese people moving between Hong Kong and the mainland reaching five to six thousand a day, it was impossible to keep a check on families bringing in mui-tsai. Many Chinese were totally against the idea of registration as they saw it as an infringement of their rights. By the end of 1927, 4,368 girls were registered with the authorities as mui-tsai, but it was unofficially estimated that there were at least twelve thousand in the colony.

The indefatigable Lieutenant-Commander and Mrs Haslewood continued to press for abolition. Their book, *Child Slavery in Hong Kong: the Mui-tsai System*, published in London in 1930, was extensively read. In a widely reported address to the annual conference of the British Commonwealth League in 1934, Haslewood condemned registration as totally inadequate. "Just before registration in 1929 the government of Hong Kong was claiming that an army of inspectors would be required with the widest powers of entry and search. Yet after it, the British Parliament was constantly told that the number appointed (three) was in every way adequate." Haslewood pulled no punches. "Slavery exists in the British Crown colony of Hong Kong today under the mui-tsai and kindred systems. No centenary celebrations of the abolition of slavery in British possessions, however numerous, will alter the fact."

The government, however, continued to hold to the protectionist line, claiming that the views represented by the eminent members of the Society for the Protection of Mui-tsai were more representative of Chinese opinion. The fact that the Anti-Mui-tsai Society had many more Chinese members seemed to be irrelevant. Unlike the protectionists, the abolitionists did not have the influential Hong Kong District Watch Committee, the Tung Wah Committee nor the Po Leung Kuk on their side.

However, to satisfy liberal opinion, the British government set up a commission of inquiry to examine the mui-tsai system at first hand in Hong Kong and Malaya. The commission, consisting of two men and a woman, arrived in Hong Kong by ship for a three-week visit in 1936. The leader of the team, Sir Wilfred Woods, was a former financial secretary in the government of Ceylon; L.A. Willis had served in the Sudan political service; and Miss E. Picton-Turberville was an ex-member of Parliament. The choice of three people without first-hand knowledge of China, Malaya or Hong Kong was presumably deliberate; they would, it was hoped, see the problem objectively. Nevertheless, the last great ideological battle over mui-tsai was fought, this time between Miss Picton-Turberville and her two male colleagues.

Miss Picton-Turberville adamantly refused to sign the lengthy report drawn up by Sir Wilfred on the basis that it did not portray the situation accurately. Instead, she drew up her own minority report, in which she accused the Hong Kong government of not doing enough to abolish the exploitation of women and girls in Hong Kong. This ran counter to Sir Wilfred's report which had expressed the view that the Hong Kong government was doing its best to solve the problem. Miss Picton-Turberville argued that the number of unregistered mui-tsai ran into thousands, far more than the few hundred mentioned by Sir Wilfred. More importantly, she felt that the connection between the mui-tsai system and prostitution was far greater than the majority report allowed.

Whatever the repercussions of the battle between Miss Picton-Turberville and her two colleagues, the British government was soon to find that it had other, more pressing, problems to deal with in Europe. The mui-tsai system, which had been dealt severe blows by the laws of 1923 and 1929, gradually died a natural death after the war as circumstances and attitudes in Hong Kong changed.

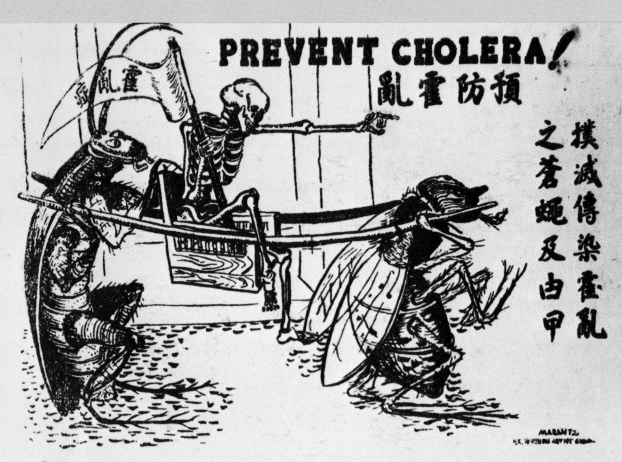

One of the six anti-cholera posters issued by the Medical Department in an endeavour to check the progress of this dread disease. The posters, in red and black, are designed especially for the Chinese masses.

15

EXPATRIATE CHILDHOOD

"The feeling then in Hong Kong was that it was an unhealthy place for children. Without air travel we didn't come back to Hong Kong for the holidays and I saw my parents together only once during the whole time I was at school."

Michael Wright

Although there were schools for expatriate children in Hong Kong, most children were sent off to boarding school in England. As the sea journey out and back took so long there was no time to come out even in the long summer holidays, and parents might be separated from their children for years.

Peggy Beard's parents left her behind at boarding school in England when they returned to Hong Kong in 1919 at the end of the World War I. "It didn't seem to be the thing to stay at school here," she recalls. "I didn't see my parents for three years. I spent holidays with my grandparents. You just accepted it. It was the normal thing to do."

Harry Owen Hughes was sent away to boarding school for ten years and hardly knew his father when he returned to join the family business in Hong Kong in 1918. "A splendid fellow", was Harry's verdict on his father, but for many others the distance created between parents and children by sending them away to school was one that would never be breached.

One alternative was to send children to boarding school in China where the weather was cooler and the opportunity of being together during the holidays greater. Many went to a school in Weihaiwei run along English lines.

Peter Potts was sent to a prep school in Tsingtao called St Giles. His parents chose it mainly for its good year-round climate.

For those children who did stay in Hong Kong there were compensations. Michael Wright enjoyed the Peak School until he was packed off to England at the age of nine in 1921. He and his brother were taken up to the school (the building now houses the Peak fire station) by sedan chair. He remembers their market coolie delivering two scooters to the school every day so that he and his brother could freewheel on the traffic-free roads back down to their house on Coombe Road. The boy next door had a donkey. He was taken up to the Peak School by sedan chair but the donkey was taken up by a servant every day so the boy could ride home.

Malcolm Swan had a very full life at Taikoo dockyard. "You could play badminton, billiards, table tennis, lawn bowls, walk in the hills around or swim in the harbour off the dockhead at Taikoo. There were launch picnics in the summer run by the dockyard to Big Wave Bay or Clearwater Bay and sometimes we'd be in company with a launch picnic from Kowloon dock or the naval dockyard. Things were very cheap. For a dollar I could go to the pictures and have a drink and a slab of chocolate cake afterwards. We'd go to the Queen's or King's Theatres in Central or the Oriental in Wanchai, though the King's was better as it was the first to have air-conditioning. People smoked a lot and they used to close the shutters, so there was practically no ventilation and you had two hours of agony in the summer."

The dockyard had its own rifle range in the valley running up from Quarry Bay to Mount Parker, and there were summer quarters for Taikoo families at the top of the gap between Quarry Bay and Tytam. Malcolm Swan loved moving up there with his family in the hot season and especially the cable railway ride up in a car which was open at the sides and had only a rope and a hook to prevent people from falling out. The summer quarters were fairly primitive. There were no flush toilets, only thunderboxes; Malcolm Swan remembers being woken up at night by the coolies who came up to empty them. But being up there was, in the mind of a child at least, idyllic. He even enjoyed going to church on Sunday. Union Church on Kennedy Road was the Taikoo dockyard church and every Sunday a launch would run from the dock to Queen's Pier transporting the congregation in their Sunday best. From Queen's Pier they walked up Garden Road to church. What Malcolm Swan liked about it was the fact that church parades for the troops were compulsory. "A Scottish battalion in Murray Barracks would go to Union Church and an English battalion to the cathedral. To march behind them with their bands, especially when it was a Highland regiment, was a terrific thing to do and made going to church a pleasure, even for a small boy."

The Central British School was located between the Miramar Hotel and St Andrew's Church in Nathan Road before being moved to its present site in Kowloon Tong in 1935. To get there from Taikoo, Malcolm Swan took a launch to the public pier at Tsimshatsui and then shared a rickshaw with another boy up Nathan Road for ten cents between them. As its name implies, Central British School was exclusively for British children. Eurasians and Chinese went to Diocesan Boys' or Girls' Schools and the Chinese had

Queen's and King's Colleges. The Diocesan Boys' School's playing fields were in King's Park. School uniform was strict and formal, with jackets and ties even in summer, but no caps. Malcolm Swan remembers the headmaster, Reverend Upsdall, constantly lecturing on the responsibilities of being a member of the great British empire and the duty of all students to uphold the white man's burden in "darkest Hong Kong".

How threatening was Hong Kong to the well-being of children? Peggy Beard's mother, whose own father had been a doctor, was so terrified of plague and smallpox that she rarely took her daughter into Central, except for a special reason like getting a dress fitted at Madam Flint's in Queen's Road. Perhaps at the back of her mind was the great plague of 1894, which would still have been a major talking point when she first came out to Hong Kong at the turn of the century. If Hong Kong no longer suffered its earlier reputation of being a "white man's grave", there were still outbreaks of dreaded disease in the colony, and the South China Morning Post daily reported the number of cholera and small-pox deaths.

The Sino-Japanese War did nothing to allay fears about public health in Hong Kong. As fighting impeded the supply of vegetables and meat into Hong Kong, prices went up and the ordinary Chinese became more under-nourished than ever. Massive numbers of refugees coming into Hong Kong brought smallpox, cholera, dysentery and typhoid fever. In 1939 there were four thousand reported deaths from tuberculosis in Hong Kong; many more went unreported. Smallpox and cholera reached epidemic propor-tions in the winter of 1937-38 with 1,800 dying of smallpox and, in one week alone, over two hundred of cholera.

Although the epidemic mainly affected the Chinese population, expatriates were not entirely immune. Four Europeans went down with cholera in the week beginning 21 August 1937, including the editor of the Hongkong Telegraph. Expatriate fears increased when it was discovered that the

John Beard and governess, 1932.

Peter Potts on Redwings, Fanling, Boxing Day, 1938.

John Beard with toy rickshaw, Kowloon, 1930.

one thing the four Europeans had in common was that they had all tiffined at the same time in the fashionable Café Wiseman. There were shudders of disbelief when it was suggested that cholera could have been transmitted through iced consommé julienne, poached fillet of garoupa, roast spring chicken, rissoles, kale au beurre and caramel custard, the tiffin menu for that day. Business fell drastically at the café for a few days, although the management defended itself by saying that 144 tiffins had been served that day, that the victims had been seated at different tables and had been served by four different waiters.

The case for sending children away to school was further strengthened later that year when the colony suffered an outbreak of Shiga dysentery. Forty-seven expatriate children went down with the disease in eleven days in November 1937 and eight died. The discovery that all of the children had drunk milk from Dairy Farm led to an investigation into standards of hygiene there, and a new policy was introduced by the management to pasteurise all Dairy Farm milk.

Fear of disease apart, there were sights in Hong Kong from which parents felt their children should be protected. By 1935 there were nearly a thousand lepers roaming the streets, a number sufficiently high to prompt the setting up of a special committee to look into opening an asylum in the New Territories "to protect the public from distressing spectacles due to the revolting nature of the disease in its advanced stages and the horror with which it is commonly regarded". As an interim measure destitute lepers were herded together into a dilapidated building of the former Tung Wah Smallpox Hospital, surrounded by barbed wire and kept off the streets by a special police patrol.

The refugee influx from the war in China also brought a fair crop of lepers into Hong Kong. Forty were sent back across the border to a leper colony in Swatow, but most of them felt that life was so much better for them in Hong Kong that they suffered the twenty-day walk back to the colony on ulcerated feet after the Japanese bombed Swatow.

Expatriate parents also had an underlying fear that the Chinese, however law-abiding they might seem, might rise up against them. Many expatriates living in Hong Kong had direct experience of the general strike of 1925. Fears for their children's safety reached fever pitch in June 1934 with the story that five young expatriate children, innocently playing near the lower Peak Tram station, had been thrown bodily into a nullah by a "crazed Chinaman". It had been raining heavily, sending water cascading down the nullah. Four of the children, aged between five and eight, managed to scramble out of the raging torrent, but eight year old Michael Paine, the only son of a master gunner stationed at Victoria barracks, was swept underground. His battered body was fished out of the sea near Victoria Recreation Club by a Private Kelly, who, seeing the boy disappear, had grabbed a rickshaw and dashed down Garden Road to where the nullah entered the harbour.

The murder trial that followed confirmed for many expatriates that their children were better off at school in Dorking or Cheltenham, even if it meant that they would rarely see them, as children, again.

16

THE JOURNEY HOME

"On the day when a popular resident leaves there is a steady stream of flower bearers heading for Queen's Pier and the ferry. The departing woman feels for once in her life like a prima donna or film star, while husband follows with parcels of chocolate, lavender water and books. Friends pour on to the launch or ferry and then on to the P & O or Empress boat, which becomes a seething mass of humanity and flowers. Coolies fight their way up the gang-plank with countless baskets of flowers. Drinks are ordered wildly on board, but often don't appear until the seers-off have gone and anchors are aweigh."

Under the Mosquito Curtain, *Lady Bella Southorn*

In the days before fast air travel the usual method of returning to England for Home leave was by steamship. Adventurous travellers might take the Trans-Siberian railway or, in the late 1930s a flying boat Home, but for most expatriates out from England, five weeks on a ship was part and parcel of living in the Orient. For those prone to seasickness the journey was a nightmare, but for people who enjoyed spending weeks on a floating hotel, the experience was unforgettable.

As Home leave was a rare occurrence, those leaving by ship were given a tremendous send-off from Kowloon Wharf. Farewelling was a major social occasion — one saw off friends, colleagues and acquaintances or just went along for the party. P & O ships sailed from Hong Kong on alternate Saturdays and, amid the streamers, brass bands, waving crowds and sweating coolies, there were usually a few shroffs' agents trying to secure payment for chits which departing passengers had forgotten to honour. For shopkeepers and hoteliers it was often the last chance

to secure payment in a society in which credit was automatic; but, as Marjorie Angus recalls, they were often unlucky, because "once the propeller turned, all debts were automatically cancelled".

Once on board, passengers could finally settle down to a cruise via Singapore, Penang, Colombo, Bombay, Aden, Port Said, Malta, Marseilles and Gibraltar which would last five glorious weeks before coming to an end at Tilbury docks in London.

Eighteen year old Edith Starling wrote a series of letters to her mother as she sailed Home on the P & O liner *Rawalpindi* in the spring of 1938. She, like many single girls in Hong Kong, was working her passage as a nanny. Her charge was a boy named Robert, who was being packed off to boarding school at the early age of three. The ship ran straight into a typhoon. "I was amused to discover that after dinner the only people on deck were Mr and Mrs B., two other ladies extremely seedy and about four other couples dancing and

"Flower Street" (Wyndham Street), 1937.

P & O ready to sail from Kowloon Wharf, 1928. The party is over and now comes the rather tedious time of waiting while the ship builds up steam and prepares to cast off. As the whistle blows, the band on board strikes up, streamers are thrown in both directions and final farewells made.

South China Morning Post, *1936.*

Farewellers await the departure of an ocean linear, Kowloon, 1928. Some of those in the picture may have been in what Lady Southorn called the PSOC (Professional Seers-Off Club).

The party on board HMS Medway, *1932. On the right of this photograph is Gertie Simmonds; fourth from her left is her sister Kathleen. Although acclaimed as beauties, the fact that their mother was Japanese destroyed their chances of good marriages in a society in which an "officer and a gentleman" would lose his job if he married an Asiatic.*

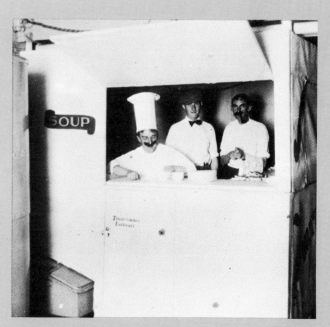

Refreshments provided by courtesy of the soup kitchen, HMS Medway, *1932.*

South China Morning Post, *1934.*

133

myself, and that out of a total of seventy first-class passengers! I went to bed at 11.00 p.m., and it was very rough during the night and some of the passenger cabins were flooded, and the wind was terrific, a proper typhoon wind, and the siren kept blowing, for you couldn't see your hand before your face."

Once sea conditions settled, passengers got down to the serious business of organising their own entertainment. An entertainment committee was formed to arrange dances, parties, competitions and fancy dress and passengers each contributed a small sum to pay for prizes.

The evening before the liner docked at Singapore, there was frog-racing at 9.15 p.m. "All the second-class passengers were invited to our deck and it made quite a jolly crowd. Frog-racing is really a gambling game and at the word 'Go', you have to pull a string with a wooden frog attached, and the one who gets their frog home first wins. It sounds very simple but the wretched frogs refused to stand up half the time, or else couldn't be made to move and it was really very exciting, especially as there was quite a lot of money bet on the different favourites. I got talking to a rather nice young man from the Singapore air force during the game and afterwards I was asked to join his party at a table by another young man. At midnight they all wanted to go for a swim, but I didn't much want to so went to bed at about 12.30 instead . . . . There isn't any need for me to flirt, dear Ma, the men come flocking without me raising a finger; I have a swimming date with a nice Irishman at 7.30 p.m.!"

Romance flourished in such circumstances. Marjorie Angus recalls that in the Red Sea she was taken on to the top deck and shown the Southern Cross. "I was taken there twice in one night and they were both wrong."

The comparative calm of the Red Sea provided much-needed relief for those who suffered sea-sickness in the more open seas before and after Suez. Leslie Ralph's wife was a bad traveller, "but she was very fond of champagne and her cure for seasickness was champagne and a biscuit. I'm not sure if she was as sick as she pretended to be. She certainly drank a lot of champagne."

For children, life on board meant the freedom of the decks, organised games and a swimming pool. Malcolm Swan made his first voyage at the age of eight on board the P & O *Rajputana*. "We travelled second class, which didn't bother us children as we ignored the class barriers. The swimming pool was a great canvas bucket slung up on deck and filled with sea water. It was reserved for children in the afternoons until four o'clock, when we had to make way for the grown-ups coming on deck from their afternoon sleep. If we weren't swimming, the deck steward used to round us up at two o'clock and lock us in the nursery until four. It was either into the pool or into the nursery between two and four, because the afternoon siesta for grown-ups was sacred."

WE'LL LOOK AFTER YOU ON THE

P & O

AGENTS:— **MACKINNON, MACKENZIE & CO.**

South China Morning Post, *1938.*

Regimentation on board was particularly a feature of the P & O ships. Michael Wright remembers the strict rules of P & O with mixed feelings: "You had to go down to dinner at the right time and if you were late you missed it. It never worried me because I was so jolly hungry that I did get down at the right time. But some people who liked a lot to drink before meals didn't like the P & O. The only thing I had against

the P & O as compared to Lloyd-Triestino, for instance, was that when we travelled with our Chinese amah she was regarded as something very foreign. She wasn't allowed to have meals with our children or with us and had to eat standing up in the corridor. On the German *Norddeutscher Lloyd* not only was she treated like an ordinary human being, but rather better. A German stewardess brought her food on a tray in our cabin.''

Fancy dress was as much a feature of any voyage as it had been of social life back in Hong Kong. Edith Starling had neither the imagination nor the motivation to put much effort into her costume, and attended fancy dress night as a flower girl, having borrowed a shawl, a pair of earrings and some artificial flowers. Others were more exotic. "The man at the next table was a scream. He is an enormous man and very tall and he was dressed as a 'Glaxo Baby' with pink ribbons in his hair and a frilly dress on and his wife went as his nurse. Several of the younger men were dressed in the stewardesses' uniforms and looked very comical, and the big Scotsman behind my table was dressed in a travelling rug with bottles of Scotch whisky dangling from his belt. The first prize for the most original lady's dress was awarded to a lady in a black, hooded costume with a hangman's noose dangling over her head and a half-empty bottle tied to her dress with a notice which read 'The Last Drop'. Very clever, I thought. The most original man's prize went to 'Herr Hitler'. Dancing began and continued till about 3.00 a.m. Everyone looked dead the next day but it was great fun."

Fancy dress dances could have their embarrassing moments, as Leslie Ralph discovered in the Suez Canal: "I went to Simon Arzt and bought the worst tie they had in stock to go as an American tourist. Back on board I went down the lift to dinner before the dance, and in came somebody dressed exactly as I was, except that he wasn't in fancy dress."

Edith Starling's charge Robert went to a children's fancy dress party as a Chinese boy. Having been placed in the care of a total stranger

Fancy dress aboard a P & O, 1934.

Life on the first-class deck, P & O, 1936. Moonlit nights in the Red Sea were especially conducive to romance as enough distance had been covered either way for people to get to know one another. Many a young woman coming out to get married in Hong Kong would fall for the charms of a Malayan rubber planter or a chief petty officer on the way and get off at Penang or Singapore instead.

Deck games aboard a P & O in the Red Sea, 1934.

P & O, 1928. On many ships swimming pools were rather unglamorous makeshift affairs rigged up for passing through the warmer climes.

*Simon Arzt,
Port Said, 1927.*

in an unfamiliar setting, he was proving to be so difficult that Edith often felt like "throwing the brat overboard". At the fancy dress he "refused to walk and sprawled across the track and screamed", having earlier hit Edith in the mouth with all his strength, at which "several people muttered unpleasant things about him and Mrs B. told me to 'take him for a walk'. He only settled down after receiving a consolation prize and pieces of a cake made by the chef for 'future empire builders'."

Apart from screaming children and heavy seas, another source of discomfiture was getting caught on or near the ship at a coaling station. The newer steam ships burned oil, but the older ones burned coal and had to refuel at a number of ports. Malcolm Swan remembers leaving the ship at Aden, Colombo and Port Said and seeing "from a distance, clouds of coal dust floating in the air. Everything on the ship was battened down but the dust sifted through. As soon as the ship put to sea the crew scrubbed it down from top to bottom."

At Suez, a party left the ship to visit the Pyramids and the Sphinx at Giza. The minimum price in 1938 was £7-7s-6d, which Edith Starling thought was too much to pay for one day's sightseeing. It also meant missing the trip through the canal. "We simply crawled along and it was great fun waving to the Sunday trippers who were

bathing along the banks of the canal, and some of them had their tents erected under the shade of trees. We all had to keep our sunglasses on for there was a strong glare from the sand and we found the flies rather trying. At night the landscape assumed the aspect of an Arabian Nights fantasy. The silence of the surrounding desert wrapped in sleep, the magic of the stars and the brilliance of the powerful search-light in the bow of the ship made the night seem darker and accentuated the fantasy."

At Port Said in the morning, all was hustle and bustle. The water was too shallow for a big boat to anchor off the jetty; as soon as the boat was made fast it was surrounded by bumboatmen selling all kinds of wares – Turkish Delight, baskets, North African poufs, Arab hats, beads, and dirty postcards from Casablanca. First on board was the Gully-Gully Man, a dusky gentleman who pulled chickens from out of breast pockets, from under the arms and out of the ears, and performed other feats of magic with expert sleight-of-hand. He maintained a fast patter, "No cheeken, no ra-bbit, no mon-goose", interspersed with "gully-gully".

Malcolm Swan was always most impressed by the service at Simon Arzt, the famous Port Said emporium. "A Simon Arzt man came on board ship when you arrived at Port Said, carried off your dirty summer linen in a trunk and had it

South China Morning Post, *1939.*

South China Morning Post, *1939.*

South China Morning Post, *1936. Blue Funnel travel was not quite as expensive as P & O and many preferred its more democratic atmosphere.*

ready for you all washed and pressed on your way back from leave, months later. If they had rented it out to someone else in the meantime you never knew the difference."

The *Rawalpindi* left Port Said at 11.00 p.m. An hour before sailing, the Cairo day-trippers rejoined the ship "all looking very tired and grubby," according to Edith Starling. "It wasn't until the next day that you got any sense out of them — and how they talked! They all pretended to be very stiff after their *very* short ride on a camel."

It was now full steam into the Mediterranean, which was pleasant in summer but chilly in winter. For passengers like Edith Starling, a few years in Hong Kong had thinned the blood and May in the Mediterranean felt very cold.

A stop at Malta took her mind off the temperature. "I thought it the most romantic looking place I have ever seen. Little boats were plying from land to the ship and it looked like a bit of Venice for they are built like gondolas and rowed by swarthy Italians ... We went ashore at 9.30 a.m. and I was thrilled to see the Hovis bread carts and the absence of anything Eastern."

Marseilles was next and passengers who were in a hurry to get back to England, or wanted to avoid the Bay of Biscay, disembarked for the train to Paris and Calais. Malcolm Swan, though, could never understand those who opted to travel overland. "I thought people who did that were mad; to give up a week on board ship was my idea of utter foolishness. By the time you got to the Bay of Biscay you'd got your sea legs, especially if you had survived the China Sea in the north-east monsoon. Coming the other way you went straight into the bay from Tilbury, so that was very different."

The P & O passenger liner Rajputana *on her maiden voyage, 1925.*

In her last letter to her mother, posted at Plymouth, Edith Starling reported the rigours of Biscay. "We entered the bay at 8.00 p.m. this evening and the ship has been pitching up and down all day. Mrs B. has lost her tiffin and tea and there have been several corpses strewn around the deck this afternoon. I am pleased to say that I have not been seasick once during the whole voyage. The only thing I don't like about it is that I can't find anybody for a game of ping-pong."

The *Rawalpindi* arrived at King George V dock in London at 7.00 a.m. on Friday, 3 June, thirty-six days after leaving Hong Kong. Within two years the ship, like others in the P & O Eastern service, was converted into an armed merchant cruiser following the outbreak of World War II. A few months later, she was sent to the bottom after engaging in unequal combat with the German battle cruisers *Gneisenau* and *Scharnhorst*. The *Rajputana* served on convoy duty in the north Atlantic, escorting more than seven hundred ships without loss until, in April 1941, she was torpedoed by a U-boat 250 kilometres south of Iceland.

17

PLANES AND TRAINS

"We must envisage a very definite growth in air traffic and air-mindedness. With established air-routes it will be much easier for businessmen and others to pay short visits to the Far East. The more wealthy classes of tourists and holiday-makers may well be induced to visit Hong Kong and China if they can do so without the need of a long sea journey."

Government report, 1935

Air travel was still very much in its infancy at the end of World War I. The first sustained heavier than air flight had been made by the Wright brothers in 1903. Louis Bleriot crossed the English Channel solo in half an hour six years later. World War I provided a great stimulus to aeronautical engineering and by 1919 Alcock and Brown had made the first direct flight across the Atlantic. Sir John Alcock was killed in an air crash shortly afterwards, but Sir Arthur Brown lived on to preach the gospel of flying. In 1920 he visited Hong Kong as part of an American team organising the First Aerial Derby Round the World and spoke to the Chamber of Commerce. Like most air enthusiasts he saw the future for Hong Kong in terms of flying boats rather than conventional aircraft. Rocky Hong Kong could not support an airstrip, while flying boats required only a pier and a landing stage tower. The chairman of the Chamber of Commerce supported the idea, adding that Hong Kong, as one of the largest shipping ports in the world, should do all it could to ensure that what she had become to those who went down to the sea in ships, she should also become to those in the future who went up in the air in ships.

The early years of aviation in Hong Kong were not entirely auspicious. To inaugurate a new commercial air company on Chinese New Year's Day in 1925 one Reg Earnshaw made a parachute jump on Kai Tak, missed and was drowned in the harbour. It was later discovered that the fire-crackers which had been tied to the plane's tail on take-off had been rubbed in the dust and failed to go off.

However, in spite of such bad *joss*, aviation in Hong Kong steadily grew. Governor Cecil Clementi was an enthusiastic supporter, and it was his initiative that led to the founding of the Hong Kong Flying Club in 1929. On 1 November 1928 local aviation history was made when four flying boats flew in from Singapore. In 1930 the Legislative Council voted a grant to support the new industry, but it was another six years before Kai Tak airport was regularly used for commercial flying. In those days the runway crossed the road which ran from Kowloon to the Saikung peninsula. According to the Raven Sisters, "You had to wait until the plane landed or took off, then they would pull up the wooden gates across the road to let your car through."

In March 1936 the flight from Penang to Hong

First Siberian Mails for a Fortnight.

The first mail from Home and Europe *via* Siberia arrived late on Monday evening on the s.s. *Altai Maru*. This mail was discharged early yesterday morning, and was ready for collection and delivery by ten o'clock. On enquiry at the General Post Office yesterday there was no information available as to why this mail had been held up for so long. The mail was dated London, June 18th. The total number of bags landed here was 403, of which 62 contained letters and papers from the United Kingdom, and 72 had mail from Europe. This mail was followed by the arrival early yesterday morning of the s.s. *Carnarvonshire* from the North, which brought, in addition to Shanghai mail, mail from Home and Europe *via* Siberia. This mail totalled 134 bags, of which there were 48 bags of papers only from the United Kingdom. There is another United Kingdom and Europe mail due in this week *via* Negapatam; this being expected by the s.s. *Santhia* on Saturday. Letters and papers on board are dated London, June 16th.

Mail sent via Siberia was quicker in theory, but often slower in practice than the regular steamship routes. Quite often it disappeared altogether.

142

Kong was inaugurated, linking Hong Kong to London by air. A year later Hong Kong residents were able to fly to London for the coronation, courtesy of Imperial Airways. The ten-day trip was considered unbelievably short by those accustomed to steamship travel. In that same year Pan America started up a Manila-Hong Kong service, which linked Hong Kong with San Francisco, six and a half flying days away. By 1938 the number of passenger arrivals at Kai Tak had almost trebled to nearly ten thousand.

Leslie Ralph was an early passenger on a flying boat to London. "Those were the days when you were treated as a VIP if you travelled by air. It was more expensive than the ship, but the firm paid the equivalent of a first-class steamer fare and I paid the difference. A speedboat from Central steps took us out to the flying boat lying at anchor. At the first stop, Bangkok, a speedboat met us and took us to a hotel, where we spent the night. Rangoon next, then somewhere in India, then to Sharja in the Persian Desert, where we spent the night in a Beau-geste fort. From there we dropped down on to the Sea of Galilee. Next it was Genoa, and finally home to Plymouth. It was lovely to stop overnight in a good hotel, even better than a ship."

The cost of air travel before the war nevertheless remained prohibitive for most people. Even though the prices of air fares were beginning to fall by 1938, the trip to London cost £160 single and £288 return compared to the return steamship fare of £70 second-class and £105 first-class.

The only other means of reaching Europe available to those who disliked sea travel or wanted to halve their travel time was to take the Trans-Siberian railway. Before the advent of an air service between Hong Kong and Europe, letters and parcels would be stamped "Via Siberia" if they were to be sent overland. Unfortunately, mail could often go astray due to the turbulent political situation in Russia and China at the time.

Some people loved the journey in spite of its potential hazards. Ten year old Peggy Hookham, for instance, thoroughly enjoyed the experience

South China Morning Post, *1937.*

143

of fourteen days on the train, with its lush velvet interiors and samovars steaming away on wood-burning stoves. She wrote glowingly of the trip in her autobiography, *Margot Fonteyn*.

The Trans-Siberian was always more popular with residents of Shanghai than Hong Kong, partly because for them a sea voyage took much longer. However, from 1937 onwards passengers could board a train in Hong Kong and, with only a few changes of carriage, step off the same train at Victoria station in London eighteen days later. Locomotives and carriages were transported across the English Channel on a Calais-Dover ferry. Tickets for the entire journey, bookable through Thomas Cook, cost between £27 and £57 one-way in 1939.

The Chinese authorities had for years refused to build a line linking the Kowloon-Canton rail-way to the Trans-Siberian, as they feared that the transport of goods directly between central China and Hong Kong would put Canton out of business. They only bowed to the inevitable after the Sino-Japanese War broke out in 1937 and the blocking of the Yangtze River by the Japanese army made Hong Kong the only port through which their supplies could pass. However, the Japanese occupation of Canton made through-journeys virtually impossible.

Like most Hong Kong residents, Leslie Ralph never much liked the idea of a journey home by rail even when it was possible to travel from door to door. "It was a tiring trip and the trouble was that whenever there were squabbles in the north, you had to travel for long distances with the blinds down, so you couldn't see much. Anyway, I would much rather spend five weeks at sea."

18

UP COUNTRY

"As I cannot believe that the British empire will ever acquiesce in the retrocession of Hong Kong to China, it behoves us to offer, and the sooner the better, terms upon which the Chinese can honourably agree to the cession of the New Territories in perpetuity to Great Britain."

Sir Cecil Clementi, 1936

When those words were written, Britain's ninety-nine year lease of the New Territories, acquired from China in June 1898, still had over sixty years to run. Even so, the nationalist government of Chiang Kai-shek had made enough noise about Britain's extraterritorial rights in China, and the "unequal treaties" made by the former Manchu rulers, for those in high places in Hong Kong to realise that one day China might well ask for the New Territories back, if not the whole of Hong Kong.

Britain had initially acquired the lease of the mainland to meet possible attack from the north — not from China, but from European powers in China. The 1890s coincided with Russian aggrandisement in the Far East, French moves into Indo-China and a bid by Germany's aggressive new kaiser, Wilhelm II, for a "place in the sun" in China. The prospect of Russian, French or German power bearing down on Hong Kong and Kowloon from the north was not one which Britain much relished, so the New Territories were acquired to serve as a buffer zone.

Getting the Chinese government to agree to the lease was not difficult; what *was* difficult was getting the Chinese villagers who lived in the area to accept their new rulers. Resistance was particularly strong in the walled village of Kam Tin. British troops drove out its 2,600 men and

captured the city's iron gates, which Governor Blake subsequently took back with him to Britain as a souvenir of his years in Hong Kong. In purloining the gates Blake had been acting in the accepted tradition of nineteenth-century British administrators. Lord Elgin's famous Marbles, taken from Greece and handed over to the British Museum, were an earlier, more blatant example of this tradition. The village elders of Kam Tin, however, never forgot the theft of their gates and continued to request their return. It was not until the 1920s that Blake's family and the government agreed, and the gates were duly reinstated at the entrance of Kam Tin walled village. Outside, the grateful elders erected a plaque, on which are described the circumstances in which the gates were taken and a brief, diplomatic account of how they were returned: "The twenty-sixth descendant, Paak Kam, representing the people of the compound, petitioned the Hong Kong government to bring the matter before London and have the gates returned and re-hung as before. All the expenses were paid by the Hong Kong government. We also thank Sir Reginald Stubbs for his presence at the ceremony; from this can be seen the deep kindness and great virtue of the British government and shows that our people are pleased and sincerely submitted, therefore we especially carve the above on the tablet, in order

Rice cultivation provided work for many of the six hundred villages of the New Territories and gave Hong Kong its staple diet.

to remember and never forget this kindness. Great Britain, May 26th 1925, Chinese Republic 14th year, on Yuet Hoi year, the 'yuen' 4th month, 5th the lucky day, we carved."

In addition to Kam Tin, there were six hundred villages and hamlets, many accessible only by sea. Rice cultivation flourished and family life still thrived — the depopulation caused by emigration to a new life in Hong Kong's factories or in the Chinese take-aways and laundries of England, America and Australia was yet to come. Nevertheless, the census of 1921 shows that the size of New Territories' families was declining as teenage boys sought work in Hong Kong and girls left to become mui-tsai in the city or *sanpo-tsai*, prospective brides, in south China.

Health standards in the villages were often abysmal, as Chinese suspicion of Western medicine was especially strong. Life expectancy was low; it was estimated that whereas in England and Wales the number of people alive at sixty years old pro-

portionate to the number born was forty-one per cent, in the northern New Territories it was only nineteen per cent.

Using primitive methods, and limited by traditional attitudes and lack of capital, New Territories farmers scraped a living which was barely at subsistence level. A New Territories agricultural association was set up to try and promote agricultural development through annual shows. The first agricultural show was held at Sheung Shui in 1927 and became an annual event attended by colony leaders and the local peasant population. The 1930 show opened to the music of the 3/15 Punjabi band and the arrival of Governor and Lady Clementi, Sir Robert and Lady Ho-tung and the New Territories elders. In his opening speech, Sir Cecil Clementi said that although he realised the New Territories would never be self-supporting in meat and rice he hoped they would become so in vegetables and wood fuel. He particularly looked forward to the future develop-

Open road in the New Territories with rice paddies on either side, 1927.

ment of pineapple cultivation in the Territories, an idea which somehow never really got off the ground, although pineapples had been grown in places like Pineapple Pass (and still do grow in a few areas today).

Lady Margaret Ho-tung had herself made a contribution to the economy of the New Territories by developing large-scale silk production at the Ho-tung farm in Sheung Shui. She and her workers had distinguished themselves at the British Empire Exhibition held at Wembley in 1924, where they won a diploma and special certificate for a silk worm exhibit which delighted English girls eager to see where their silk stockings had come from.

Exhibits in 1930 included a flower show, a range of products from ICI and examples of poultry breeding and Chinese and European vegetables. However, the major attractions at the show were models of engines and coaches provided by the Kowloon-Canton railway and models of the German cruiser *Scharnhorst* and ocean liner *Mauretania* made by a boy named Jerry Sousa.

There were few European homes in the New Territories outside Fanling and Taipo in 1920, much to the chagrin of the shareholders of the Kowloon-Canton railway, who had hoped for European settlement along the line when they opened it in 1911. The New Territories were then regarded as rather remote and potentially

dangerous for Europeans. Banditry was almost as widespread in the area as it was in Kwangtung province, and in September 1930 the colony was stunned at the murder of a European police sergeant's wife at an isolated police station in Lokmachau. An Indian police constable, Dalip Singh, had run amok, shooting at fellow officers and killing Mrs Madgwick before shooting himself. The tragedy had close parallels with one twelve years before when another Sikh policeman fired on a European sergeant and his wife and baby at the police station in Tai-O. The wife and baby survived but Sergeant T. Glendinning died, as did the killer, who turned the gun on himself.

Fanling, with its golf club and racecourse and its retreat for the governor, Fanling Lodge (opened in 1934), was popular among Europeans who kept summer bungalows there. There was also a small European community at Taipo, the leading light amongst them being a certain Mr Brayfield, the so-called "mayor of Taipo", who wrote a weekly newspaper article on the life of the community. The Chinese villagers called Brayfield "Water Buffalo". Amina el Arculli remembers him having a thing about mosquitoes and terrorising her family's *fa-wong* during his regular inspections of their flower pots to see if they were a breeding ground for mosquitoes.

Eric Himsworth recalls a feud that developed between Brayfield and the manager of the Kowloon-Canton railway. "It was the habit of

Mr Brayfield to ride his horse alongside the railway track, a habit to which Mr Baker objected as he thought it was dangerous and foolhardy. But Mr Brayfield had always ridden his horse along the railway track and refused to give up the habit, until Mr Baker had him summoned to the district officer's court in Taipo for trespassing on railway property. There was a real set-to, with King's counsels appearing in magistrates' courts, which was most unusual. Eventually Mr Brayfield said he would have his revenge on Baker and his KCR. What he did was to send a large parcel of fresh fish from Taipo to the railway terminus in Tsimshatsui, where it was put in the luggage room and left. Brayfield had timed his revenge perfectly. It was the middle of summer and a frightful smell soon permeated the whole of Kowloon railway station. Nobody came to collect it and it wasn't until the stench reached the newly built Peninsula Hotel that the fish, and its sender, were finally traced. Baker was furious, but what could he do?"

Amina el Arculli lived with her brother, two sisters and widowed father in a sprawling bungalow with a swimming pool and tennis court next to the Shatin inlet. The Arcullis had originally come out from India to provision British troops stationed in tents on Kowloon peninsula in the 1860s. Abbas el Arculli had chosen to go into law rather than the family business, and his work as a solicitor made him the doyen of Hong Kong's Indian community — he became life president of the Indian Recreation Club in the early 1920s. After his wife died he decided to leave a large house on Kennedy Road in favour of "country life" in Shatin, commuting to his office in town by train from Shatin station. The only other large houses in the area belonged to the Chans, the Ho-tungs and, at Tofungshan, the Anglican church, where Bishop Hall lived.

Amina el Arculli recalls her childhood and teenage years in Shatin before the war with a great deal of affection. "It was so quiet and peaceful and we always had plenty to do. Father taught us how to swim and to ride bicycles — there was hardly any traffic on the main road then — and we played tennis on our own court. We all learned how to shoot a .22 rifle. We had a bull's eye in the grounds and practised every Sunday. Father was a crack shot and had a hunting rifle, a revolver and the .22. Shatin was a peaceful place and we got on well with the villagers, but Father wanted us to learn the use of firearms just in case of trouble when he wasn't home . . . Electricity hadn't reached Shatin then, so we had our own windmill. For days when there was no wind we used a dynamo for the wireless, lights and a small fridge. The lights weren't very bright."

The family had ten servants: a driver drove and maintained the family car; a gardener, assisted by a coolie boy, grew vegetables, fruit and flowers; a houseboy looked after the dogs and maintained the house; a cook made the family meals; a wash amah did the washing by hand; and each of the four children had a personal amah.

"The servants called Father 'Master' and us girls 'Missie'. My brother was 'young Master Number One' and my older sister 'Missie Number Two'. As the middle sister I was 'Missie Number Three'. At dinner the houseboy served each of us individually. My father first, then each child according to age. Our personal amahs stood behind our chairs and got us to eat up. The normal practice in Hong Kong was for the children to have their meals separately from their parents but, not having a mother, we ate our meals with Father."

A close bond existed between servants and old established families like the Arcullis. "Every few years the servants would go back to their home villages in the country ('Canton more far') and would automatically find a substitute for the time they were away. There was a strong sense of mutual loyalty. Most of our servants stayed with us until they were old. Father looked after all their problems and pensioned them off when they retired. The cook, for example, was pensioned off just three months before the war, as he was getting old and frail. He went to retire in Macau and got his pension remitted to him every month. My brother's amah was still getting her pension

Homes for the very poor, New Territories, 1930.

New Territories village boy, 1927. Like most New Territories children, this boy began working in the paddy fields as soon as he could walk.

New Territories villagers at work, 1939.

New Territories village market scene, 1939.

after the war. My own amah said she would stay with us for as long as we were in Hong Kong. When Hong Kong came under Japanese occupation we couldn't pay her, but we still fed her. She came with us when we went to Macau in 1943 and after the war ended Father paid her for the four years' wages he had missed."

Amina el Arculli's amah, who joined the family when Amina was born in 1924, is still with her at the present Arculli home in Stanley in 1983.

For Europeans living in Hong Kong and Kowloon, the New Territories provided an escape from urban life and made up for the absence of frequent leaves abroad. To occupy themselves during long school holidays in the 1930s, Rosemary Parsons and her friends from the naval dockyard would travel the deserted roads by bus. Marjorie Angus remembers the pleasures of hiking over New Territories hills covered in orchids. It has been said that the sweet smell of orchids on Hong Kong's hills was responsible for its name, "Fragrant Harbour". The naturalist J.L. Young

Saye collected thirty-three species of the flower on a three-day trek over Maonshan in 1937.

The New Territories were the haunt of naturalists. Butterfly Valley, crossed by a mountain stream, was a favourite spot near Laichikok. The Chinese in Hong Kong had yet to discover the joys of hiking, camping and barbecuing, so the countryside of the New Territories was virgin territory for the European.

However, as W.L. Handyside commented in 1930, " The outlying districts of the colony are a closed book to most people, both European and Chinese. In the case of the former, knowledge of the New Territories is limited to the main motor road or the railway route to Sheung Shui, and the latter scarcely ever dream of moving far from their own district. The European schoolboy is a natural explorer, but this trait seems to be almost entirely lacking in the Chinese schoolboy. We recently heard of senior pupils in one of our local schools who had never been to Repulse Bay."

Rice paddies in the valley looking towards Amah Rock.

Marjorie Angus (front left) and friends from Kowloon, New Territories, 1929.

Sunday hike in the New Territories, 1929.

On the way to a Sunday picnic in the New Territories, 1930. After 1919 it was possible to drive on traffic-free roads in a circular route round the New Territories.

The streamlined Taipo Belle *outside the Kowloon-Canton railway terminus, Tsimshatsui, 1939.*

One intrepid hiker who strayed off the beaten track was Leslie Ralph; he regularly crossed to the New Territories at weekends from his home on the Peak. His diary for New Year's Day 1927 records a typical day out. "Reid, Orr and I walked in the New Territory from Laichikok to Taipo. I was not sure whether dogs were allowed to cross the harbour so I smuggled Patch across in a walla-walla to the Kowloon station steps. It was a glorious day but the picturesqueness of the walk was lessened by the new Shinmun Valley Water Scheme, which was interesting, however, to see for the first time. We ate our tiffin at Pineapple Pass upon which Patch was sick and we had to go slowly. She revived after a rest, but we did not have to hurry as we had ordered tea on the 5.30 from Taipo market. We returned to the mess in nice time for dinner, pleasantly tired."

Had Leslie Ralph taken the train ten years later he might have travelled in streamlined luxury parlour cars on board the *Canton Belle*, with its silver and green livery, or the silver and blue *Taipo Belle*. The cars each had armchairs, a smoking lounge, a cocktail bar, attendants and a rear observation compartment. The Kowloon-Canton railway rented them out for parties of up to twenty-four people at twelve dollars a head.

The outlying islands were rarely visited by people from the city except by private launch and were essentially the preserve of fisherfolk and villagers. Cheung Chau was the exception; a European reservation had been created there as a summer resort for "missionaries and others from the interior". Access to Lantau Island was difficult enough to put most people off. G.S.P. Heywood, however, was an enthusiastic explorer and naturalist with a fierce determination to scale Lantau Peak, at whatever cost. "Like Skye, Lantau Island is difficult of access and little visited. I can never set out for either without a mild sense of adventure. The ideal way to visit Lantau is with a private launch; if, however, you are prepared to brave the discomforts of a very early start, it is possible by taking the ferry boat to spend a long day on the island and get back to Hong Kong the same evening . . . "

19

THE FANLING HUNT

"In the mind of the average person, the idea of hunting is wrapt up in an aura of grimness and expense. Button-based women, hard-faced men, and a number of extremely rude people in fancy dress dash around the country looking for hounds and foxes. How entirely different is the reality of the Fanling Hunt."

Fanling Times

A major feature of New Territories social and sporting life was the Fanling Hunt. It had its own sporting newspaper, the *Fanling Times*, its own clubhouse, the Hunter's Arms, and from the mid-thirties ran an annual Hunt ball at the Peninsula. Patrons came from the upper reaches of Hong Kong's social and regimental life. Everything was done to simulate an English Shire Hunt, with master, whips, hounds out from England and full Hunt regalia.

The terrain and quarry, however, were another matter altogether. The hills, gullies, streams, irrigation channels and dried-up rice paddies of the Fanling area, together with the heat, provided a stiff test for the most expert of horsemen. Foxes and civet cats provided quarry in the early days, but as these animals soon learned to use the difficult terrain to their advantage, the Hunt switched to paper chases — always considered rather infra-dig — and drag hunting. Alec Hutton-Potts, an enthusiastic rider from the start who later rose to be the Hunt's master ("No hill was too steep for him, no gully too deep"), regularly dragged a sack filled with aniseed around the course.

The Hunt was started in 1924 by Dr Pierce Grove and a sharebroker, Toby Birkett, after the former was sent out four pairs of foxhounds by his brother-in-law in Taunton Vale, Somerset. Following the share market collapse in the general strike of June 1925, Birkett lost so much money that he and Pierce Grove, as joint masters, could no longer afford to keep the Hunt going, until Birkett's younger colleague, Hutton-Potts, came up with the bright idea of starting a subscription pack. A meeting of interested parties was arranged at the Potts' bungalow near Beas River and financial backing was found. In the first year there were sixty subscribers, including the Hong Kong Jockey Club, whose subscription alone paid for kennelling and maintaining the hounds.

The Hunt season, from October to April, when the paddy fields lay fallow, was observed up to the Japanese invasion of Hong Kong in 1941. Meets were three times a week, Wednesday and Saturday afternoons and Sunday mornings, and began and ended at the Hunter's Arms, where members could stay the night. Governor Sir William Peel, an enthusiastic rider with the Hunt, regularly made the newly built Fanling Lodge available for Hunt garden parties during his governorship.

The parameters of the Hunt occasionally extended over the border into China. In March 1928 the commissioner for Chinese customs, Colonel Hayley Bell, arranged a special meeting

A garden party for the Hunt at Fanling Lodge, New Year's Day, 1935.

across the border, which was only partially successful, as the Fanling hounds, used to following a drag, became confused by the large numbers of foxes available and proved rather ineffective.

Because of the growing interest in riding which the Hunt had stimulated, Dr Pierce Grove decided to build a steeplechase course and training ground at Kwanti, one and a half miles from Fanling station on the road to Shautaukok. The racecourse of six furlongs, begun in November 1925, had eight jumps 3'4" high and a water jump of 2'10" with eight feet of water, all "very strong" jumps. The course had a private stand and enclosure for subscribers to the hounds as well as a public stand and enclosure; the admission price for the latter was one dollar. Subscribers could bring in two lady guests free and a limited number of gentlemen at five dollars each. Behind the stands was the jockeys' room, *pari-mutuel* shed and bar.

Races were run under British National Hunt and Hong Kong Jockey Club rules and culminated in an annual Fanling National at which regimental bands like the 2nd Battalion Argyle and Sutherland Highlanders laid on musical interludes. On race days special race trains were provided by the Kowloon-Canton railway at reduced rates.

The mounts, as at Happy Valley, were north China ponies known for carrying heavy weights at great speed. They were mainly racing discards brought down from Shanghai and earned their keep in the off-season by serving as polo ponies at the Causeway Bay polo ground.

Leslie Ralph was a frequent visitor to the Kwanti racecourse. His diary entry for 6 February 1927 describes one Sunday outing. "Caught 10.30 a.m. train to Fanling in lovely cold weather and walked to the Kwanti course to look at the condition of the ground. Tiffined at the Hunter's Arms with Potts and several others. In the afternoon I rode Potts' horses over the jumps before going on to tea at McGowan's bungalow."

The following Saturday he was back for the races, having been up since five in the morning to gallop ponies at Happy Valley in preparation for the big four-day meeting the following month. "Caught the 1.15 train to Fanling and had tiffin on the journey with Wallam, Brodie and Eileen, who were all going to the Kwanti steeplechase meeting. I rode Two Pairs in the first race and was an absolute favourite: unfortunately, however, a silly ass ran right across the first jump, shoving me out. That apparently fed my pony up and he refused the majority of jumps all the way round before I ultimately got him over. I came in second, about two furlongs behind the first pony. In the second run I rode Craigarad, which also belonged to Alec Potts. This was a very exciting race and after a comfortable ride I dead-heated for first place. Rode Gymp, belonging to the aforesaid silly ass, in the last race, but was not placed. Went back to the Hunter's Arms for tea and caught the 5.50 train back. Dined at the mess, played bridge and went to bed."

Unfortunately, Leslie Ralph's riding days came to an end at Kwanti when he broke his pelvis, collarbone and a rib in a fall at one of the jumps.

With the incorporation of the racecourse the original Fanling Hunt became the Fanling Hunt and Race Club. The club's memorandum and articles of association are dated 7 November 1929. In the early days the club was male-dominated, but by the early thirties there were

Leading in a winner,
Kwanti, 1928.
Beryl Fair up.

Over the hurdles
at Kwanti,
1928.

The tote and enclosure
at Kwanti racecourse, 1926.

Hunters in full regalia with foxhounds, Fanling, 1935.

Hunters and friends at a Sunday meeting, Fanling, 1939. Alec Hutton Potts is front right. His photographs of the Fanling Hunt survived the Japanese occupation of Hong Kong hidden in a tin box placed in the rafters of a Kowloon godown. Unlike most other private photograph collections, they were not used as fuel.

The kennels, Fanling, 1938.

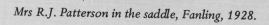

FANLING HUNT.

MARCH MEETS.

Saturday, March 3rd	Hunt Ball.
Sunday, 4th	Lincolnshire Mess, Sun Wai.
Wednesday, 7th	Lok Ma Chau.
Sunday, 11th	17 Pine Tree Hill.
Wednesday, 14th	Dills Corner.
Sunday, 18th	Kwanti Race Meeting
Wednesday, 21st	Potts Bungalow.
Sunday, 25th	Fanling Hunt Point-to-Point.
Wednesday, 28th	The Kennels.
Sunday, April 1st	Hunters Arms.

To finish the Season.

Meets at the end of March depend on the state of the land and climate.
3.00 p.m. each day.

Master.

Mrs R.J. Patterson in the saddle, Fanling, 1928.

The Hunt in full chase.

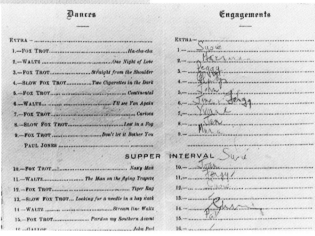

Supper

Consommé Chassepotts

Garoupa Operée par MacGowan
Prawn MacNamara
Pilaw of Lobster Georges

Cailles Stephen

Suprèmes de Perdreaux Nosworthy
Chicken and Ham aux deux B.F.
Salade St. Anton Japonaise

Kwanti-tin of Fruit
Walls Ice Cream
The Worry

Peninsula Hotel   *Le 2 Mars, 1935*

*The Hunt ball at the
Peninsula Hotel, 1935.*

*Hunt Ball
1935.*

a good number of lady riders, the most redoubtable of whom were the Fair sisters, Betty and Beryl ("the two BFs"), Joan Dowbiggin, Yvonne Shenton and Pamela Scott Harston.

The number of patrons of the Hunt and Race Club grew considerably during the thirties. Increasingly, stockbrokers, bankers, lawyers and accountants were joined by Volunteers and men from regular regiments like the King's Own Scottish Borderers, the Somerset Light Infantry, the Argyle and Sutherland Highlanders and the Royal Infantry. To bring everybody together in celebration of the club's achievements, the first of the annual Hunt balls was held at the Peninsula Hotel on 2 March 1935. Diners were offered Consommé Chassepotts, Garoupa Opereé par McGowan and Chicken and Ham aux deux BF.

The last Fanling National, run on 23 March 1941, was won by Brutus, ridden by the governor's ADC, Captain Treverton. The following Hunt season was brought to an abrupt end by the Japanese invasion in December; and after the war the New Territories changed, and chicken farms, fruit orchards and new settlements made it impossible to find the wide, open terrain a good Hunt required. The hounds vanished in the years of occupation, doubtless providing villagers with a good stew in those difficult times. Some, perhaps, survived. Peggy Beard, whose father and sister Jean rode in the Fanling Hunt, swears that if you look closely at the features of those tawdry village dogs in the New Territories today you would not be mistaken if you recognised the look of an English foxhound in one or two of them.

158

20

THE BANK : COMPRADORES AND ART DECO

"Please build us the best bank in the world."

Sir Vandeleur Grayburn to
Palmer and Turner, 1933

Most people between the wars would have agreed that the Hongkong and Shanghai Bank had long been the greatest bank in Hong Kong and the greatest foreign bank in China. Its key role in promoting the colony's emergence as a major trading centre was beyond doubt. The statue to Sir Thomas Jackson, the bank's chief manager in the nineteenth century, is evidence of the colony's recognition of this. However, in the shadows of the bank's success stood a breed of men whose low public profile, at least in European eyes, made them less well known than the taipans but whose importance in the growth of the bank was equally significant: the compradore.

Some of the richest and most prominent men in the Hong Kong Chinese community were the compradores of foreign firms. In the interwar period the bank's chief compradore was Ho Saiwing, a member of one of Hong Kong's wealthiest families and the adopted son of Sir Robert Hotung.

The compradore system had developed among foreign firms in China in response to the need to relate business to the language and practices of Oriental culture. The first compradores were recruited from the area around Macau and Canton. The Portuguese based in Macau in the sixteenth century were the first Europeans to trade in China and the word "compradore" was taken over by British traders who later set up factories in the area.

The position developed because of a fundamental difference between Western and Eastern business practice: while the West relied on signed contracts, the Chinese system depended upon personal relationships. This and the multiplicity of currency on the China coast — the tael, sycee and variously minted silver dollars — called for the expertise of a local person who understood and could communicate to foreigners the complexities of the China trade.

The compradore of a foreign company was responsible for the hiring, firing and supervision of Chinese staff and for ensuring the smooth transaction of trade with Chinese customers. The ideal compradore was a man of substance with close business and social connections in the Chinese community and a reputation for honesty, loyalty and integrity. Because he controlled large sums of money, he had to provide safe security and reliable guarantors. By 1906 the bank demanded security of a million dollars from its Hong Kong compradore having discovered to its

cost that two previous compradores had not been men of integrity.

The compradore's staff was mainly recruited by personal recommendation or acquaintance, so family and clan ties played a large part in the system. A compradore felt responsible for providing jobs for his relatives and every local position in a foreign trading hong, from the highest to the most menial, might be recruited from a single family. A 1928 photograph of the Hongkong and Shanghai Bank's compradore staff includes thirteen members of the Lau family, although it had been fourteen years since a Lau had been compradore. Five members of the 1928 staff bear the surname Wei and were related to an earlier assistant compradore, Wei Long-shan.

The compradore's monthly salary was modest — in 1920 it was $150 a month — but his real potential for income lay in the commission he received on all business he brought to the company and in private deals which his inside knowledge of the market and widespread family interests allowed. The bank's compradore, like all compradores for the mighty hongs of the East, walked a tightrope. Success could mean fabulous wealth, failure financial ruin. The temptations to

misuse large amounts of money were great and many compradores in the East succumbed to them. Ho Sai-wing's predecessor at the bank's Hong Kong office left suddenly in 1912, his affairs in disorder; the compradore before him had declared bankruptcy and the one before him had absconded.

In a community organised around business and lacking a literary tradition, the compradore became a natural leader of the Chinese in Hong Kong. His knowledge brought the Chinese an understanding of the ways of the West and, in a wider context, opened the eyes of the Middle Kingdom to the outside world. On the other hand, the compradore worked for foreigners and helped to usher in the Westernisation of China. It was his influence and knowledge which did so much to promote foreign imperialism in the East, his capital which helped to develop railways, mining and industry.

Paradoxically, the more effective the compradore system became the more it was rendered unnecessary.

The bank's compradore in Hong Kong during the twenties and thirties, Ho Sai-wing, was a member of the Eurasian community and as such

160

did not have the strong clan attachments of his Chinese predecessors. However, the Eurasians in Hong Kong had developed strong interfamily connections which Ho Sai-wing was able to draw on. His adoptive father, Sir Robert Ho-tung, had risen through the compradore ranks of Jardine, Matheson and Company to become its head compradore and was later succeeded in the position by two of his brothers, one of whom was Ho Sai-wing's natural father, Ho-fuk. Ho-fuk's other sons became compradores for the Mercantile Bank, E.D. Sassoon and Company, Jardine and Arnhold and Company.

The bank in Ho Sai-wing's time was still very traditional in many of its practices. Ledger entries by Chinese staff were made with a Chinese brush instead of pen and ink, and the abacus was used instead of the adding machine. Changes, however, were inevitable.

The educational advances of the interwar years improved the staff's standard of English, so the need to have them in a special section diminished. The narrowing of the gap between Chinese and Western business methods meant there was less need for someone with a specialised knowedge of Chinese affairs.

The Hongkong and Shanghai Bank 1883–1934.

The 1930s were a time of forward thinking for the Hongkong Bank, as symbolised by the stunning new building opened in 1935. Critics called it "Grayburn's Folly". Admirers thought it the most imposing piece of bank architecture outside America. The Japanese imperial high command considered it good enough to be the headquarters of their occupation government of Hong Kong during the war years. The new Hongkong and Shanghai Bank building in Central dominated the Hong Kong skyline until it was dwarfed by the high-rise explosion of the 1960s.

The new headquarters for the bank was the brainchild of the bank's chief manager, Sir Vandeleur Grayburn. The world-wide depression following the Wall Street crash had lowered construction costs in Hong Kong, and it was felt that the project would indirectly benefit some of the bank's more important clients — Jardine, Dodwell, Hutchison and Gilman — who were the colony's agents for building materials and equipment. Moreover, there were other, more pressing reasons. The vaults in which silver deposited with the government as security for the bank's note issues was kept had, for some time, been in a sorry state. Lack of temperature and humidity controls had caused the straw sacks containing much of the silver to rot and the treasury floor was littered with loose coins, rotting straw, cockroaches and rat droppings. The bank staff's tiffin area was located on the first floor, but the kitchens shared the basement with the treasury.

Another contributing factor was that the Shanghai branch of the bank was housed in a more imposing building than Hong Kong's old-fashioned headquarters, now fifty years old. Built on The Bund in 1923, the Shanghai building, with its lofty dome, granite façade and columns and two massive bronze lions guarding the entrance, was considered the most impressive in the city. The disturbed political conditions in China caused by the Japanese invasion of Manchuria and the activities of the communists, while they disrupted trade generally, worked to the advantage of the bank as Chinese capital flowed into Hong Kong and Shanghai for safe-keeping. Consequently, Sir Vandeleur Grayburn and his directors made the bold decision to go ahead with the building of a head office in Hong Kong which would not only rightly outshine the branch office in Shanghai, but would meet the requirement Grayburn passed on to the architects, Palmer and Turner, for a bank which would be the best in the world.

In order to achieve such an impressive goal, more land was needed. Negotiations with the government were begun and it was agreed that the bank could lease Wardley Street and a portion of the old City Hall site. As Queen's Road curved half-way along one side of the area, however, the site was not a perfect rectangle. Nor was it flat: the site sloped from Queen's Road down to Des Voeux Road, creating problems in the construction of two major entrances. Although the building's main façade would face on to Statue Square and the harbour, Grayburn insisted that preserving the bank's address of 1 Queen's Road Central meant creating an equally imposing entrance on the back side.

The bank's designer, G.L. Wilson, a senior partner of Palmer and Turner, wanted to create a building that would be familiar enough to be popular and at the same time architecturally avant-garde. L'Exposition des Arts Décoratifs et Industriels Modernes, held in Paris in 1925, provided the stimulus for the new art deco style which Wilson would use to such good effect in the interior of the bank. Wilson's other main source of inspiration came from the Moderne movement which was best represented by the latest New York skyscrapers. New Yorkers had earlier complained that high-rise buildings were turning their streets into dark canyons; this resulted in a new law which required that the upper portions of high buildings should be set back at a certain level but allowed a tower of unlimited height over the site. Thus, whereas the Shanghai branch had a dome, the Hong Kong building would have a tower similar in style to New York's Empire State Building.

Wilson had to somehow combine a symmetrical scheme which would house a traditional banking hall layout into a Moderne shell with a high-rise tower block, and take into consideration the

Art deco details.

"Podgoursky's perfection". The mosaic ceiling was generally regarded as the building's artistic masterpiece. Below it, the great Ashburton marble columns rise above a Swedish marble floor.

The Hongkong and Shanghai Bank, 1935.

peculiarities of the site and Sir Vandeleur Grayburn's insistence that the back entrance be as imposing as the front. The roof would also have to accommodate a helicopter landing pad and the tower a squash court.

The Moderne style allowed him to use a wide variety of motifs drawn from a range of sources. Sculpted heads of "men of vision" flanked by lions' heads, symbols of strength, each carved out of a five-ton block of local granite, surmounted the buttresses of the tower. Bronze lions guarded the front entrance, as at the Shanghai branch. The original designs for the Shanghai lions, which were cast in a Cornwall foundry, had been lost, so the Hong Kong lions were modelled on the Shanghai ones and cast in Shanghai as no Hong Kong firm seemed capable of making them. The main staircase landing merged heraldic lions with lamps which could be interpreted as either medieval torches or science-fiction rays. The Queen's Road entrance was protected by bronze gates topped by Norman figures in armour, suggesting a medieval portcullis.

The interior of the banking hall was surfaced with various marbles: the walls of cream Botticino marble contrasted with the dark Ashburton marble of the columns, the green Swedish marble of the public floorspace and the black Devonshire and Belgian marble of the counters. It was lit by strategically placed lighting which produced a diffuse shadowless light for the working surfaces, public space and ceiling.

The ceiling was to be the building's *pièce de résistance*, a mosaic vault made up of four million glass pieces. The Shanghai office of Palmer and Turner found a Russian emigré artist named Podgoursky to design it. Podgoursky went to Florence to work on the design with the assistance of a Professor del Zotto, while another Italian, Raoul Bigazzi, went to Venice to have the Venetian mosaic pieces made by the best mosaic craftsmen in the world.

Podgoursky and del Zotto had problems finding a place big enough to do their drawings until the Italian government stepped in with the offer of a disused church with a large enough wall

At the laying of the foundation stone in 1934 a sealed copper casket was buried containing newspapers, banknotes, coins and other bank memorabilia of the day. The casket was retrieved intact following the demolition of the building in 1982.

These coins were retrieved from the casket under the Hong Kong Bank's foundations in 1982. The silver one-dollar coin was used as trade currency and was barely in circulation. After the outbreak of the Sino-Japanese War, silver and copper coins were smuggled out of the colony and into China by the thousands. The Hong Kong government had to replace the coins with notes.

Japanese sumo wrestling medal, 1943. So impressive was the bank building that it was taken over by the Japanese military administration as their headquarters during the war years.

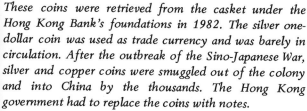

The old bank building featured on most Hongkong and Shanghai Banking Corporation banknotes of the period.

The only banknote to feature the new building before the war.

area on which full scale drawings could be made. The finished drawings were then sent up to Venice where the coloured, gold and silver mosaic pieces were glued on to them face down; the full-size drawing was then cut up like a gigantic jig-saw puzzle, each piece numbered according to a master plan, then carefully placed into the hold of a ship bound for Hong Kong. Under the super-vision of Bigazzi, the ceiling of the banking hall was covered with well-levelled and smoothly coated cement and the mosaic pieces, still attached to the drawings, were pressed on to it in the order shown on the key plan. When the cement was dry, the drawing was removed with brushes and water and the mosaic tiles rubbed down with muriatic acid. The six-month job of applying the mosaic to the ceiling was done by Chinese workers, mostly from Shanghai, who had never done anything like it before.

Podgoursky's creation, a pastiche of classical, modern industrial and commercial, Oriental and Western themes reflected the spirit of his age. The poet W.H. Auden wrote rather unkindly that the bankers had "erected a worthy temple to the Comic Muse". Podgoursky's ceiling bore little relation to the purpose for which the new bank was erected. Most who entered the banking hall paid little heed to the mosaic's story. Nevertheless, the ceiling was the largest of its kind in the Far East and the second largest in the world, and nobody who did their business under it, however hurriedly, could avoid being moved in some way by its magnificence.

Grayburn came under fire for spending so much money on what many shareholders con-sidered to be an unnecessary luxury. Conse-quently, he hesitated when it came to the expensive question of whether or not the bank should be air-conditioned, in spite of the fact that the earlier Shanghai branch had had air-conditioning installed. In his view, the new invention had yet to prove itself, but he was eventually swung over to the idea by the Shanghai commissioner of public health, who wrote to the bank saying, "My own impression is that air-conditioning on the whole tends to diminish disease and certainly renders the staff very much more comfortable and more able to do work efficiently throughout their periods of duty. I am also of the opinion that the fact that air-conditioning is growing all over the world indicates the need for some such procedure."

For Sir Vandeleur Grayburn the opening ceremony on 10 October 1935 was a proud moment. The building, like the men behind it, reflected confidence in the future and stood as a monument to the commercial flair which had made Hong Kong one of the great trading cities of the world.

But no institution lasts for ever. Within eight years the tall, imposing Grayburn was to die from meningitis and sceptic boils in Stanley Internment Camp. The bank's compradore, Ho Sai-wing, died in 1946 from the effects of imprisonment and maltreatment suffered during the Japanese occupation; the term "compradore" was abolished in 1960. And in 1982 the building itself fell to demolition squads and man's need to meet the challenge of the future — a need which Sir Vandeleur Grayburn would have recognised and understood.

21

WAR CLOUDS : 1937 - 1941

On the fruits of sweating coolies' toil
They lived their complacent lives,
And on the eve of battle
We still heard them prattle,
"Why don't they send us back our wives."

Shamshuipo POW camp ditty, 1942

It could be said that World War II effectively broke out in July 1937 when the Japanese attack on Peking heralded the beginning of the Sino-Japanese War and an attempt to bring the whole of the Far East into a Japanese-dominated East Asian Co-prosperity Sphere.

In August 1937 the Japanese began their bombing of Shanghai, leading to the greatest influx of refugees into Hong Kong since the Taiping Rebellion in the 1850s. Within a year a quarter of a million newcomers were walking the streets of Hong Kong, putting intolerable strain on the colony's already overburdened housing situation and bringing with them bad health and variable skills. With thirty thousand sleeping on the streets, the government was forced by the summer of 1938 to set up refugee camps at North Point, Kowloon Tsai and King's Road. When the camps became full, railway wagons were used as additional accommodation for refugees in Fanling until new camps could be opened.

Landlords, taking advantage of the demand for living space, raised the rent on bedspaces and cubicles to such a degree that the government had to give tenants twelve months' protection against eviction.

The fall of Canton to Japanese troops in October 1938 brought the war closer to Hong Kong and further increased the numbers of Chinese seeking refuge in the British Crown colony. The massive influx raised the question of unrestricted right of entry into Hong Kong, and from then on all Chinese had to have entry passes, frontier passes or residential certificates. Emergency regulations, last enforced in 1931, were revived by the government to give the police power to arrest vagrants, search without a warrant and banish from the colony anyone who did not have a job. Meetings, processions and organisations suspected of sedition were forbidden, and censorship was imposed over Chinese newspapers, placards and pamphlets.

As the fighting steadily engulfed south China the supply of meat and vegetables into Hong Kong was blocked, making a poor public health situation worse. Refugees brought with them smallpox, cholera, dysentery, typhoid and leprosy. In 1939 four thousand died of tuberculosis, according to official figures, although there were many more unreported deaths, and over three thousand suffered from beriberi.

The refugees flocking in from China were mostly of the coolie class, although there were exceptions. Some were prosperous Shanghai businessmen whose wealth and expertise enabled them to set up factories in Hong Kong. Some were Shanghai bar girls and dance hostesses who saw better opportunities for business in Hong Kong, while others were writers and journalists whose arrival in Hong Kong produced something of a Chinese literary renaissance in the colony.

A different category altogether were the British women and children evacuated from Shanghai following the Japanese attack in 1937. Some resented the term "refugee", preferring to be called "evacuees". This prompted the chairman of Hong Kong's Shanghai Refugee Committee to say, "From the point of view of Shanghai they have been 'evacuated' from that port, but to the Hong Kong mind they have taken 'refuge' in Hong Kong."

The first batch of one thousand arrived aboard the SS *Rajputana* on 19 August 1937 and were mostly accommodated by friends, relatives or their husbands' firms. The *Empress of Asia* sailed in with thirteen hundred more, followed by two more ship-loads. Others came in on special trains from Hankow in December and January, following the city's take-over by Japanese forces. Their arrival in Hong Kong coincided with a massive cholera epidemic, while the first batch from Shanghai had been hit by the devastating typhoon of 1 and 2 September, one of the worst in the colony's history. The British community in Hong Kong rallied to the cause and gave every support. More than five hundred refugees were given a temporary home in the grandstand of the Hong Kong Jockey Club in Happy Valley, with catering provided by Lane, Crawford, while others were given shelter in the new Central British School in Kowloon Tong and in "superior" camps at Shamshuipo and Laichikok. The Ohel Leah Synagogue took in orthodox Jews who wanted a strictly kosher diet. The refugees were given free passes on trams and taken on sightseeing tours round the island. Messrs Wallace Harper and Company laid on a chauffeur-driven car for them, while private individuals loaned their own cars through a car bureau operated by two ladies and took parties of refugee children to the beaches.

Officers and men of the Royal Navy laid on special dances aboard ship, the Lady Cake Shop donated two hundred cakes, a Mr Stafford-Smith provided three thousand free cigarettes and a public-spirited hairdresser named Lizzie from Tester's Beauty Parlour devoted a whole Sunday to cutting children's hair. Kowloon residents gave bedding, toys, books and wireless sets to the refugee centre at the Central British School; Whiteaway Laidlaw department store sold them warm winter clothing at half price. Mothers with babies were provided with rattan prams and amahs by the refugee organising committee, and a special school for refugee children was set up in Kowloon Union Church.

Their stay in Hong Kong was meant to be temporary, and most returned to Shanghai once the bombing there stopped and British ships were able to call in again. The colony was generally well-pleased at the support it had given the refugees, although the chairman of the Refugee Committee was sorry to report that there had been considerable thieving by them and that a good number had returned to Shanghai without paying the three dollars-a-day board and lodging fee to the camps in spite of signing promissory notes to do so. Such behaviour was considered rather "un-British", but it was recognised that their standards might have dropped owing to the proximity of Japanese aggression.

The "yellow peril", meanwhile, was coming dangerously close to Hong Kong's borders. Eight Japanese fighter planes bombed and machine-gunned a Kowloon-bound train south of Canton in October 1937. Although only two Chinese were injured, the fact that the engine and most of the damaged wagons and coaches belonged to the British section placed the Hong Kong government in a quandary. Japanese planes flew over Lantau on bombing missions to Canton, and Chinese warships lay within Hong Kong territorial waters in Mirs and Deep Bays. The war was getting too close for Hong Kong's comfort, but there was little she could do by way of remonstration as neither China nor Japan were officially at war with each other and the British government, in view of the deteriorating situation in Europe, was loath to drive Japan on to Hitler's side.

At the outbreak of war in China, there were

over a thousand Japanese residents in Hong Kong, most of them running bars, shops and massage parlours in Wanchai or living in comparative style in large houses on Kennedy and May Roads. Local feeling against the Japanese in Hong Kong ran high following the Japanese attack on China, especially after the air raids on Canton. Stories of Japanese atrocities against their brethren on the mainland inflamed Chinese nationalist sentiment, which was further fuelled by rumours of poisoned foodstuffs being distributed in Hong Kong by Japanese agents and news of the sinking of ten Chinese junks by a Japanese submarine in Hong Kong waters.

Nevertheless, there were few overt expressions of anti-Japanese hostility among the local population, apart from the smashing and looting of Japanese shops in Wanchai and the beating up of some northern Chinese who had been mistaken for Japanese. Hostility was expressed in other ways. A twenty-five year old man appeared in Kowloon magistracy in January 1938 on a charge of demanding with menaces a hundred dollars from a factory foreman whom he had accused of selling scrap iron to Japan. An angry crowd gathered near Queen's Pier on a Sunday afternoon and threatened to kill two Japanese men who had become involved in an argument with an Indian policeman and knocked his turban off his head. It was not often that Chinese crowds came to the aid of turbaned Indian policemen, but these were special circumstances. The Japanese consulate cautioned its nationals not to venture on to the streets on the anniversary of the Shanghai bombings.

In 1938 the government refused permission for Sun Yat-sen's widow to use the ZBW studios to broadcast an emotional plea to the American people to boycott Japanese trade and to cease supplying the scrap iron used in Japanese shells to "destroy the people of China" on the grounds that the appeal would be too inflammatory. The government also arranged for special police patrols to stand guard outside Japanese shops, hotels and homes and at night concentrated Japanese residents into buildings in Central, Western and Kowloon for their protection. Nevertheless, over half the Japanese in Hong Kong, fearing the worst, shut up shop and left the colony, leaving behind a hard core who combined their regular jobs with work as secret agents. The headquarters for Japanese espionage in south China, Malaya and Hong Kong was the bogus King Chung Company (China Development Company) based in Shameen, Canton, a subsidiary organisation of the South Manchurian railway whose salaries and expenses were paid directly by the Japanese war ministry. Their agents in Hong Kong were thought to be attached to the Japanese consulate and operated out of offices in Macdonnell and Kennedy Roads.

Japanese agents worked as waiters, barmen, hairdressers and masseurs, or at any trade in which customers were given to sharing confidences. Japanese bars in Wanchai were among the most popular in town. A pint at Nagasaki Joe's was ten cents cheaper than anywhere else and the girls in Japanese bars seemed especially solicitous. A Japanese professor wrote later that "there were at that time some brave Japanese girls who had patriotic duties to perform. They went about their duties silently and methodically." Above all, they listened. Equally silent, methodical and given to listening was Hong Kong's finest hairdresser, a Japanese who had in seven years cut the hair of two governors, the commissioner of police, the officer in charge of Special Branch, the colonial secretary and the chairman of the Hongkong and Shanghai Bank. Following the colony's capitulation on Christmas Day 1941, he presented himself to his former customers in the uniform of a commander of the Imperial Japanese Navy.

The head of Japanese intelligence in Hong Kong was Colonel Suzuki, seconded from the imperial army for the purpose of learning English. His chief source of information on British military arrangements was the Chinese triad society, Kao Ki-kan, whose members had found work with the British military authorities. In return for huge pay-offs by the Japanese, filtered through Suzuki, the triad members passed

South China Morning Post, *late thirties. Miss Takamura, for one, was known to be a Japanese spy who passed information gained from clients to her boss, Colonel Suzuki.*

Hongkong Telegraph, *1939. The photograph from a German newspaper shows a coolie smoking a pipe beside the sedan chair waiting area on Wyndham Street. The German caption, in translation, reads, "This is the way in which nations are being poisoned, an example of the mess in England's colonies: Chinese coolie smoking opium pipe openly in Hong Kong street." To which the* Hongkong Telegraph *responded, "The pipe, of course is an ordinary Chinese tobacco pipe and is used for no other purpose. Thousands of coolies use them openly in the streets, just as Germans use their meerschaums if — like the Chinese coolie in Hong Kong — they can get tobacco now in Germany!"*

A Bird's-Eye View

By Argus

Every encouragement is being given to refugees to leave Hongkong. Tell me, what do I have to do to become a refugee?

* * *

The League of Nations has been informed of Germany's aggression against Poland. But talking to yourself is a bad habit.

* * *

By order, bouquets of flowers must not be thrown at Herr Hitler. Or if they are the lucky horseshoes must be taken out first.

* * *

A lad was taken for an aeroplane ride to cure his whooping cough. Another way is to visit a town that's being bombed.

South China Morning Post, *1939.*

back information on British defence positions, a military communications chart, copies of ammunition returns, transport figures, artillery positions and a rundown of the exact number and quality of troops who would oppose a Japanese attack should the Japanese cross the border. A year after his arrival, an astute British Intelligence officer discovered that not only had Suzuki learned no English, but that he was in fact amassing detailed information on Hong Kong's defences and infrastructure. The governor was informed, but the wheels of bureaucracy turned slowly and it took three months before the decision to expel him was made. The British government stepped in, however, and refused to offer such a grave affront to Japan at a time when the two countries were not in a state of war.

Suzuki stayed on in Hong Kong, continuing to enjoy regular dinner dates at the Parisian Grill and attending numerous cocktail parties, until voluntarily leaving the colony at the end of November 1941, just two weeks before the Japanese attack. When the attack finally came, most Japanese officers crossed the border carrying detailed battle maps of Hong Kong, including all its defences, and a complete order of battle. "In the variegated history of war," said Tim Carew in his book *The Fall of Hong Kong* "no army ever attacked with such explicit information about their enemy."

Britain's declaration of war against Germany on 3 September 1939 was generally met with subdued approval by the British residents of Hong Kong. Sensing that war was imminent, there was in the week before its outbreak "an air of subdued excitement in hotel lobbies and lounges and the only topic of conversation was the situation in Europe". People were on the move to get back to Europe either to join the action or merely to escape from the British colony. Passport offices were packed and large crowds milled in banking halls to withdraw their money or buy gold dollars; one man wrote a cheque for 1.3 million dollars in return for gold.

The *Overland China Mail* reported on the day after Prime Minister Chamberlain's announcement, "Hong Kong last night received news of Great Britain's declaration of war on Germany without much manifestation of feeling other than a sense of profound relief." There were, however, a few wild outbursts of national sentiment. Several parties were held at the Gripps with patriotic songs and toasts "to the damnation of Hitler", and in King's Park the swastika flying atop the German clubhouse was torn down and publicly burned. An inventory was taken of all drinks in the German Club, which was then sealed off by police, together with all other German property in the colony. Over a hundred local German men were rounded up peacefully and interned on the top floor of La Salle College in Kowloon. The internees were later joined by Czechs who had previously registered with the German consulate and changed their passports to German ones after Hitler's absorption of their country into the Third Reich in 1938. Excluded from internment, though, were those Czechs who had refused to recognise the German "protectorate" imposed on their country; and fifteen German Jews were released from La Salle after declaring they had "no love for the Nazi regime".

The Germans proved to be model internees and, as public opinion in the colony was generally sympathetic to their plight, their incarceration behind La Salle's walls — now reinforced with barbed wire, sentry towers and searchlights — was not protracted. By the end of 1939 only thirty were still there, the rest having been released to employers who vouched for their good behaviour.

Painters were kept busy in the week following the outbreak of the European war splashing red crosses on to the rooftops of hospitals and schools. The east and west Lamma channels were closed to shipping; the government fixed prices of essential foodstuffs and prohibited trading with the enemy; the vice-chancellor of Hong Kong University became the colony's chief censor.

The outbreak of war in Europe had other effects on Hong Kong. Solomon Bard, a medical student at Hong Kong University, immediately signed up for the Hong Kong Volunteers to "do my bit for the war effort", even though his finals were only three months away. The contract to build a new Government House near Magazine Gap, complete with an Italian garden and air-raid shelter, was cancelled on 8 September despite the fact that workmen's huts had already gone up on the site. The tourist trade from Europe came to a standstill, leaving hotels like the Peninsula with too many empty rooms. The order for the colony's first double-decker buses had to be cancelled as Britain was unable to supply them, and British cars were soon in such short supply that the government had to step in to curb the inflation in second-hand car prices and relax an import ban on foreign cars coming into Hong Kong.

The outbreak of the European war coincided with Japanese forces leaving Hong Kong's border. Many in Britain and Hong Kong believed, or hoped, that Japan would make a pact with Britain in retaliation against Hitler's non-aggression pact with Russia. Now that she was herself at war in Europe, it was vital for Britain not to provoke Japan into threatening her colonies in the Far East. Particularly worrying was the anti-Japanese activity organised by nationalist Chinese in Hong Kong through Kuomintang General Wu Te-chen, who worked out of Shell House, and the chief director of the South-west Printing and Publishing Company in Des Voeux Road. There was little, however, that Britain or Hong Kong could do, as local Chinese feeling was strongly nationalist and anti-Japanese and to take action against any manifestation of anti-Japanese activity was politically dangerous.

The Japanese resumed military activity on the Hong Kong border in 1940. On 29 June they retook Shataukok and imposed a blockade along the frontier. In view of the deteriorating situation, the Hong Kong government announced a policy which was to cause it a great deal of trouble right up to the day of the Japanese invasion. On the advice of the Foreign Office in London, the governor, Sir Geoffrey Northcote, made a shock announcement on 28 June 1940 that European women and children were to be evacuated from the colony. The evacuation was to be compulsory and would take place the following week.

There were to be no exceptions, except for women in nursing or other essential services. Women without children could volunteer for auxiliary nursing, and a number of women were exempted from the order as government and the hongs discovered that they could ill afford to lose their typists. Leslie Ralph's wife left, but he knew a lot of wives who became nurses overnight. "I knew one lady who put all her money and valuables in a belt around her middle and when she asked to be a nurse they said, 'Do you think you should in your condition?' " In the end she was accepted, but like so many others later regretted it. In retrospect, Leslie Ralph was glad his wife left, though not at the time. "I thanked God every day of my life while I was a prisoner (in Shamshuipo) that I had sent my wife away, though I must admit that as time went on after they had gone and nothing happened I was trying to get her back."

Isa Lammert stayed behind. She had a job in the filing department of the Hongkong and Shanghai Bank, and a boyfriend besides. Ken Watson was an up-and-coming young banker whose personal appeal, as far as Isa Lammert was concerned, far outweighed the advisability of evacuation. She was determined to stay even though her mother and younger sister left. Her decision seemed to turn out for the best, in spite of having to look after her father and doing a ninety-six hour stint as a trainee nurse at Kowloon Hospital. She and Kenneth Watson were married in St John's Cathedral and, after a very brief honeymoon at the Repulse Bay Hotel, Kenneth left Hong Kong in his capacity as an officer in the Volunteer "Wavy Navy" (the Hong Kong Royal Naval Volunteer Reserve) to pilot a tug-boat to Aden. Permission to marry, in spite of not having completed his celibate ten-year contract with the bank, was granted to Kenneth under threat of resignation. The newlyweds eventually began married life on his return to Hong Kong in

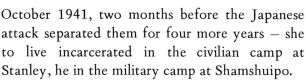

October 1941, two months before the Japanese attack separated them for four more years — she to live incarcerated in the civilian camp at Stanley, he in the military camp at Shamshuipo.

The *Empress of Asia* stood ready and waiting to sail from Kowloon Wharf on 5 July 1940, exactly a week after Governor Northcote's announcement. Among the evacuees who assembled in lines outside the Hong Kong Hotel that day were Dorothy and Winifred Raven and their mother, who were forced to leave Mr Raven to his architectural work and censor duties at Cable and Wireless. Winifred takes up the story: "It was a stuffy hot day and after we got on board they sent us down below into the steerage. Dorothy piped up, 'What do you think we are, cattle?' We went on deck and told the purser we weren't going down in those conditions. He said, 'Wait until the ship sails and we'll see what we can do for you.' We ended up in a first-class cabin. It was just as well because I was ill all the way."

At that point they knew they were going to the Philippines, but had no idea they would then be taken to Australia, a piece of intelligence they later acquired from street urchins in Manila. They spent three months in Manila, housed with other evacuees in the badminton hall of the British Club. The two sisters were never short of escorts at the all-male club. "We had a glorious time and were not for a moment down in the dumps as we got taken out nearly every night. One night we made ourselves most unpopular when we brought the mosquito nets down on everyone asleep on their canvas beds. It was three o'clock in the morning and we tripped over a rope which held the nets suspended from the ceiling. Well, what could you expect after a night on the town?"

Dorothy could have returned to Hong Kong: her boss at Imperial Airways, where she worked as a secretary, had made the necessary arrangements, but out of deference to her mother, she refused the offer. The sisters and their mother were given a warm reception when they arrived at Sydney and, after initial billeting in an evacuation centre, found a small flat at Rushcutters Bay. The girls both got jobs and soon settled into Australian life. Although they had no idea how long they would stay there, they were sure they would see their father again even though the only news they had of him after the Japanese occupation was a wartime photograph of him in Stanley Internment Camp which appeared in a Sydney newspaper.

The cost of transporting 3,500 evacuees to Australia was met by the Hong Kong government. The Australian government agreed to meet expenses for their stay in Australia at the weekly rate of fifty Australian shillings a week for women, fifteen shillings for the first child, ten for the second and five for each additional child. This money was to be reimbursed by the families concerned and the grant was to be extended only until November 1940. The Raven sisters were convinced the Australian government did not much care for the evacuation in spite of the warm welcome they received. "We didn't think the Australians were all that keen to have us. They said the first lot were so helpless, so used to having everything done for them by servants, that by the time the last boat-load arrived the Australians had had enough."

The people who had really had enough were the men left behind in Hong Kong. Governor Northcote faced a torrent of criticism from the so-called "bachelor husbands". Why, they asked, were a few thousand British women evacuated while hundreds of thousands of Chinese women remained? Why did it all have to be done so hastily? Why were American and French women not ordered to leave by their governments? Why had over 950 British women been exempted? Why was evacuation necessary at all?

The angry husbands formed themselves into an Evacuation Representation Committee, led by the dean of St John's Cathedral, the Very Reverend J. Wilson, to fight the government over the evacuation. They were supported by the Hong Kong Chamber of Commerce, which declared evacuation to be "entirely unjustified by the present situation". One woman who had returned from Manila contested the evacuation proceedings in the Supreme Court but lost.

The government stood firm. The only concession the governor made was to announce on 6 November 1940 that there was to be no further evacuation.

The arrival in September 1941 of a new governor and a new garrison commander — without their wives — did little to assuage the "bachelor husbands". Sir Mark Aitchison Young, Sir Geoffrey Northcote's replacement, told ZBW listeners in an introductory broadcast that he had thought it wise, in view of the existing international situation, to leave his wife and daughter in Ceylon. Major-General Christopher Maltby likewise left Mrs Maltby in England. Nevertheless, a fortnight after Sir Mark's ZBW broadcast the husbands held a protest meeting at the Peninsula Hotel in which a Sydney newspaper was quoted as saying that the Far East political situation had improved and that wives were rejoining their husbands in Singapore. The husbands were so irate that they considered writing letters to the outside world complaining about the tyrannical edict which deprived them of their women, but were dissuaded from doing so by the suggestion that the world, engulfed as it was in the most terrible war in history, might not be all that interested.

Besides, the Hong Kong government had other things on its mind. Rice prices had been frozen at the outbreak of the war in Europe, but the cost was still too high for many of the poor. Undernourished and overworked, they fell victim to illness and disease, and the incidence of beriberi and pellagra soared in 1940-41. The price of firewood was fixed at a dollar for forty catties, but even so there were over six thousand convictions in one month alone for cutting down trees and stripping unoccupied houses of furniture. In 1941, paper notes were issued to replace copper one-cent and nickel five- and ten-cent coins which were being smuggled into China. The government threatened to impose a full income tax, but the occupation came before the threat could be carried out.

Hong Kong was Britain's first colony to follow the mother country's example in introducing conscription. In July 1939 compulsory military service was introduced for British subjects of European birth. The ranks of the Volunteer force — both the Hong Kong Volunteer Defence Corps and the Hong Kong Royal Naval Volunteer Reserve — were swelled with new men aged between eighteen and forty-six years. Willing veterans above the age limit formed an additional group to "undertake static guard duties of vulnerable points" under A.W. Hughes, the manager of Union Insurance. The group, nicknamed the "Hughesiliers" or "Methusaliers", later became renowned for their gallant and bloody defence of the North Point power station.

The Volunteers had remained essentially British since their founding in 1855, but a Portuguese company was added in 1924 and a Chinese company introduced in 1938. The recruitment of Chinese Volunteers raised fears among those in the colony who believed the Chinese might turn on the British. Such fears had led to the disarming of Chinese police during the general strike of 1925 and the subsequent employment of more Indians and Russians in the police force. But with the Japanese advancing into south China the Chinese had to be involved in the colony's defence. Besides, they would, in the words of a *South China Morning Post* editorial, learn "discipline and character building under the right sort of officer", develop that "something about a soldier" which would inspire a new sense of civic responsibility, and be useful as a means of tapping rich Chinese for financial support.

According to Solomon Bard, the Volunteer Force "was one of the few institutions in Hong Kong where the gap between the races did not exist. While in training Chinese and Europeans were as one. Only when the uniforms came off did the barriers return." Having himself lived and worked with Chinese as a student at Hong Kong University, Solomon Bard was amazed to discover that there were British Volunteers who would refuse even to recognise their Chinese comrades-in-arms if they met out of uniform on the street.

Leslie Ralph had signed up in the Hong Kong

Royal Naval Volunteer Reserve, which had been formed by members of the Yacht Club on Trafalgar Day 1933. After the European war broke out, navy work took up more and more of his office and leisure time, and, when his family was evacuated to Australia, Leslie Ralph decided to live fulltime on board ship. He nearly lost his life at the hands of the Japanese well before the occupation, however: "I was on boom defence patrol at the Lyemun entrance into the harbour when a Japanese vessel came in. I went out to it for routine investigation, climbed the rope ladder to board the ship, inspected the captain's papers and gave him the code signal which would let him through. My boat was a small harbour launch with a canvas awning held up by spiked stanchions. As I stepped on to the rope ladder to go back, it took up the slack and I plunged down between the Japanese vessel and the launch. It was very infra-dig for a naval officer to be put in the drink like that. Besides, I missed impaling myself on the stanchions by inches. I got my own back on him when he came out because instead of being quick and efficient I was very slow. He missed the tide and ended up stopping over in Junk Bay."

Meanwhile, back on shore the government was preparing for a land and air attack. By 1939 four million sandbags were in store, eight extra "turncocks" had been trained to turn off the colony's water supply and a quarter of a million copies of the bilingual booklet, "The Protection of Your Home against Air Raids", distributed.

"Gas masks for everyone who wants one" became the slogan of the Air Raid Precautions people. At $2.50 each the British-made masks cost fifty cents more than at home, so cheaper ones were turned out by a Kowloon factory for the coolie class. They were distributed from centres set up in schools, and the face-pieces kept in airtight boxes containing nitrogen to protect them from the heat and humidity of the Hong Kong summer. The *Overland China Mail* voiced widespread criticism of what it considered to be the overemphasis on gas precautions, arguing that the Spanish Civil War had shown that gas bombing of a large city was prohibitive — to

which officialdom replied that the enemy would not use it if they knew Hong Kong were prepared.

Air-raid sirens were installed around town. "Not loud enough," cried critics who advocated the rewiring of street lights so they would sound a bell. Periodic blackouts were a mixed blessing. All external lights, including shop and club advertising signs, had to be out. Vehicle head-lights could not exceed seven watts and shone through two-inch apertures. The front glass of all lamps had to be obscured by a double thickness of blue cloth or paint. Tram cars and ferries stopped. Ships in the harbour put all lights out. The director of Air Raid Precautions, Wing Commander A.H.S. Steele-Perkins, claimed in 1939 that Hong Kong could be blacked out within three minutes, although air observers reported two years later that Hong Kong in a blackout was "a mass of lights", notwithstanding the ten-cent fine imposed on a coolie for striking a match.

Blackout practice was all very well in case of night attack, but not much use in daylight raids. More protection was needed. English-style Anderson shelters were considered unsuitable for a colony in which most people lived crowded together in tenements, and the government resisted early demands that it build underground air-raid shelters for the masses. Nevertheless, pressure from the Chinese unofficials in the Legislative Council, the press and the Kowloon Residents' Association, together with renewed fears of a Japanese attack in the summer of 1940, caused the government to change its mind. Accordingly, a massive programme of tunnel building was begun, leading to a scandal of staggering implications.

The urgency of building tunnels to accommodate half a million people in the shortest possible time, with millions of dollars involved, provided unlimited opportunity for graft and corruption, especially in the architectural branch of the Air Raid Precautions Department. The Hongkong and Shanghai Bank discovered that it could black out its entire headquarters in Queen's Road Central for one sixth of the cost allocated to it by the

Air Raid Precautions office. When the bank reported this fact to the government, the department's architect was called before a special commission of inquiry in August 1941 to explain the irregularity. The man shot himself instead, while a colleague in charge of the tunnel building was admitted to hospital with acute poisoning. The commission of inquiry proceeded to reveal corruption on a grand scale.

The government had agreed to pay costs plus ten per cent commission on contracts for Air Raid Precautions work and the purchase of stores. It was discovered that contractors had been buying heavy equipment for their own use and charging it to the government (plus ten per cent) as air-raid construction work. Ephemeral firms sprang up under different names but on the same premises and under the same boss. Materials, including dynamite, were stolen and resold; eight million sandbags bought for nearly a million dollars were found to be virtually useless. The supervisor of a Chinese construction firm admitted that he sub-contracted transport work to other firms, including one run by his wife which had no lorries. But the most sensational revelation was that Wing Commander Steel-Perkins had a very attractive Chinese girlfriend, Mimi Lau, who also happened to work for one of the contracting firms. Her firm was one of three which secured the contract for making breeze blocks. When the professor of civil engineering at the university tested a sample, only forty-six out of a hundred stood up to the specified pressure of fifteen hundred pounds. From that day on, pre-cast concrete breeze blocks were known in the trade as "Mimi Laus".

In the event the air-raid shelters, which had cost the government so much money and turmoil, were barely needed because the shelling and bombing of built-up areas were never as heavy as expected. And the commission of inquiry's report on the scandal was never made public. It was taken into Stanley Internment Camp by the commission's presiding judge and disappeared without trace after his death in the camp in 1944.

In spite of such skullduggery it was clear that the colony was prepared in its own way for war, even if the precise date and manner of a Japanese attack were uncertain. For some time there hung over Hong Kong an air of inevitability about war, even though the "bachelor husbands" did not seem to see it that way and social life carried on much as usual in the crisp sunny days of late 1941. When Japanese troops finally crossed into the New Territories on the day of the attack on Pearl Harbour, Monday, 8 December 1941, few were caught off guard.

John Stericker sensed that the balloon was about to go up on the Saturday night. He called in at the Gripps to join the usual throng in Bessie's Bar, "when a page came around the tables ringing a bell and holding up a blackboard. On that board was a message calling all merchant navy seamen and officers back to their ships immediately. As a result, thirty-two merchant ships out of some thirty-six in port got clean away to safety." Returning to his room at the hotel in the early hours, he found luggage strewn about the passageway. It was being hastily removed from the two rooms of his temporary neighbours, Madam Sun Yat-sen and the correspondent of *The Times*."

Later that Sunday morning church parade was held as usual in St John's Cathedral, with contingents from every unit in the colony marching in to the pipes of the Royal Scots and the brass band of the Middlesex Regiment. The first lesson, read by General Maltby, was taken from the Gospel of St Matthew, Chapter eight. In it, a centurion expresses doubts about his worthiness in the presence of Jesus. "For I am a man under authority, having soldiers under me; and I say to this man, Go, and he goeth; and to another, Come, and he cometh; and to my servant, Do this, and he doeth it."

Maltby returned to his pew for the singing of 'Praise My Soul the King of Heaven' but was called outside by a tense-faced staff officer. Japanese troops were massing north of Fanling. During the service senior officers left in twos and threes in response to urgent whispers from orderlies and despatch riders, as General Maltby quickly summoned an emergency conference of all unit commanders. The result of the conference was simple and straightforward: every soldier, sailor, airman and member of the Hong Kong Volunteers would be at battle stations by five o'clock that evening.

Thirteen hours later, thirty-six Japanese imperial fighters roared across the sky towards Kai Tak and in five minutes had destroyed Hong Kong's entire air force; three obsolete torpedo bombers and two antiquated amphibians. Meanwhile, Japanese troops crossed the Shumchum River for the invasion of Hong Kong. Eighteen days later, the battle was over. After sweeping through the New Territories into Kowloon, the Japanese crossed over to the island on 18 December and forced Governor Young to announce the capitulation of the British Crown colony on Christmas Day 1941.

8 December 1941 marked the end of an era. For those incarcerated in civilian or military camps, the sybaritic life of pre-war Hong Kong faded into a dream. For the Chinese masses outside the camps who had far less to lose, Japanese rule in wartime conditions proved to be far worse than British rule in peacetime.

After 1945 prosperity returned with the post-war economic miracle built on British administrative skills and Chinese ingenuity and muscle. But one thing was certain: the old attitudes of British colonial superiority and disdain for the natives were deeply shaken. And the Chinese of Hong Kong had, in seeing Britain defeated, developed an awareness that European power was no longer invincible.

As the physical shape of Hong Kong changed with the massive post-war influx of people, the rush to reclaim more land from the sea and the upward growth of multistorey buildings, so too did the collective way of thinking. The hard lessons of recent history had encouraged a little more tolerance, a little more realism and, above all, a realisation that nothing is immutable, not even life in colonial Hong Kong.

"Its leading characters are wise and witty;
Substantial men of birth and education,
With wide experience of administration,
They know the manners of a modern city.

Only the servants enter unexpected;
Their silence has a fresh dramatic use;
Here in the East the bankers have erected
A worthy temple to the Comic Muse.

Ten thousand miles from home and What's-her-name,
The bugle on the Late Victorian Hill
Puts out the soldier's light; off-stage, a war.

Thuds like the slamming of a distant door:
We cannot postulate a General Will;
For what we are, we have ourselves to blame."

Hong Kong 1938 *W.H. Auden*

BIBLIOGRAPHY

A. Primary Sources

(1) Correspondence between the Governor and the Colonial Office, London.

C0129/498/1	C0129/516/7	C0129/544/14
C0129/498/2	C0129/516/5	C0129/550/6
C0129/498/14	C0129/518/9	C0129/551/13
C0129/504/11	C0129/521/2	C0129/550/10
C0129/505/3	C0129/521/7	C0129/555/16
C0129/506/8	C0129/522/6	C0129/562/23
C0129/509/15	C0129/532/4	C0129/563/15
C0129/510/2	C0129/532/6	C0129/563/17
C0129/513/5	C0129/533/10	C0129/564/1
C0129/514/2	C0129/539/3	C0129/574/3
C0129/514/3	C0129/539/4	C0129/580/3

(2) Sessional papers of the Hong Kong government.

Reports on

Census, 1921	Census, 1931
Child labour, 1921	Praya East Reclamation, 1931
Housing, 1923	Housing, 1935
Opium, 1924	Trade depression, 1935
The port of Hong Kong, 1924	Lepers, 1935
Bathing beaches, 1926	Tourism, 1935
Boycott, 1926	Mui-tsai, 1935
Typhoon, 1926	Opium, 1935
Bias Bay piracies, 1927	Public health, 1937
Sunning piracy, 1927	Museums, 1937
Vehicular ferry, 1928	Prisoners, 1937
British Empire Exhibition, 1928	Shanghai refugees, 1937
Opium, 1928	Teachers, 1938
Opium, 1929	Labour, 1939
Mui-tsai, 1929	Air Raid Precautions, 1939
Playing fields, 1930	

(3) Newspapers.

China Mail
The Hong Kong Daily Press
Hong Kong Observer
Hongkong Telegraph
Hong Kong Weekly Press
Overland China Mail
South China Morning Post

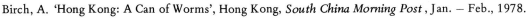

B. Secondary Sources

Birch, A. 'Hong Kong: A Can of Worms', Hong Kong, *South China Morning Post*, Jan. – Feb., 1978.

Briggs, T. and Crisswell, C. *Hong Kong. The Vanishing City*, vol. 2, Hong Kong, South China Morning Post, 1978.

Carew, T. *The Fall of Hong Kong*, London, Pan Books, 1963.

Cheng, I. 'Women Students and Graduates' in B. Harrison (ed.) *University of Hong Kong: The First Fifty Years, 1911-61*, Hong Kong University Press, 1961.

Cheng, I. *Clara Ho Tung. A Hong Kong Lady, Her Family and Her Times*, Chinese University of Hong Kong, 1976.

Chiu, T. N. *The Port of Hong Kong. A Survey of Its Development*, Hong Kong University Press, 1973.

Chung, R. 'A Study of the 1925-26 Canton-Hong Kong Strike-Boycott', MA thesis, University of Hong Kong, 1969.

Clementi, C. 'The Future of Hong Kong', *Crown Colonist*, 1936.

Coates, A. *Mountain of Light*, London, Heinemann, 1977.

Collis, M. *Wayfoong. The Hongkong and Shanghai Banking Corporation*, London, Faber and Faber, 1965.

Crisswell, C. N. *The Taipans. Hong Kong's Merchant Princes*, Hong Kong, Oxford University Press, 1981.

Crisswell, C. N. and Watson, M. *The Royal Hong Kong Police, 1841-1945*, Hong Kong, Macmillan, 1982.

Dorling, T. *Pirates*, London, Hodder and Stoughton, 1929.

Endacott, G. B. *The History of Hong Kong*, London, Oxford University Press, 1958.

Endacott, G. B. *Hong Kong Eclipse*, edited and with additional material by Alan Birch, Hong Kong, Oxford University Press, 1978.

Endacott, G. B. and Hinton, A. *Fragrant Harbour. A Short History of Hong Kong*, Hong Kong, Oxford University Press, 1962.

Endacott, G. B. and She, D. E. *The Diocese of Victoria. A Hundred Years of Church History, 1849-1949*, Hong Kong, Kelly and Walsh, 1949.

Feldwick, W. (ed.) 'Present Day Impressions of the Far East and Prominent and Progressive Chinese at Home and Abroad. The History, People, Commerce, Industries and Resources of China, Hong Kong, Indo-China, Malaya and Netherlands India', London, Globe Encyclopaedia Company, 1917.

Fonteyn, M. *Margot Fonteyn*, New York, Alfred A. Knopf, 1976.

Forbes, G. I. 'Plague in Hong Kong, 1894-1929', *Far East Medical Journal*, vol. 5, December 1969.

Gandt, R. *Season of Storms. The Siege of Hong Kong 1941*, Hong Kong, South China Morning Post, 1982.

H. H. G. and H. R. R. 'Angling in the Far East', Hardy's *Anglers' Guide*, 1929.

Gittins, J. *Eastern Windows – Western Skies*, Hong Kong, South China Morning Post, 1969.

Graham, J. *The Lowe-Bingham Story, 1902-1967*, Hong Kong, Lowe, Bingham & Matthews, 1978.

Grantham, A. *Via Ports. From Hong Kong to Hong Kong*, Hong Kong University Press, 1965.

Han Suyin *A Many Splendoured Thing*, London, Jonathan Cape, 1952.

Handyside, W. L. 'The New Territories of Hong Kong', in F. J. de Rome, N. Evans and E. C. Thomas (eds.), *Hong Kong Naturalist*, 1930.

Haslewood, H. L. *Child Slavery in Hong Kong: The Mui-tsai System*, London, Sheldon Press, 1930.

Heywood, G. P. S. 'Hong Kong Hills', *Hong Kong Naturalist*, 1936.

'Historical and Statistical Abstracts of the Colony of Hong Kong, 1841-1930', Hong Kong Government Printer, 1932.

Hong Kong Land Company Limited. A History, Hong Kong, The Company, 1975.

Hong Kong, Hong Kong, Publicity Bureau of South China, 1924.

Hornell, W. W. *The University of Hong Kong: Its Origins and Growth*, Hong Kong University Press, 1925.

Hughes, R. *Hong Kong: Borrowed Place – Borrowed Time*, London, André Deutsch, 1968.

Jarrett, V. H. G. 'Old Hong Kong', Hong Kong, *South China Morning Post*, 1933-35.

Kotewall, R. 'Confidential Report on the General Strike'.

Lau, E. 'The Role of the Hong Kong Woman in Society during the Interwar Period', unpublished BA dissertation, University of Hong Kong, 1982.

Leeming, F. *Street Studies in Hong Kong*, Hong Kong, Oxford University Press, 1977.

Lethbridge, H. *Hong Kong: Stability and Change*, Hong Kong, Oxford University Press, 1978.

Luff, J. *Hong Kong Cavalcade*, Hong Kong, South China Morning Post, 1968.

Luff, J. *The Hidden Years. Hong Kong 1941-1945*, Hong Kong, South China Morning Post, 1967.

Maitland, D. *The Peninsula Anniversary, 1928-78*, Hong Kong, The Peninsula Group, 1978.

Mattock, K. *This is Hong Kong. The Story of Government House*, Hong Kong, Government Information Service, 1978.

Maugham, S. *The Painted Veil*, London, Heinemann, 1949.

Ogden, B. 'Podgoursky's Perfection', *The Hong Kong Group Magazine*, 11, 1977.

Olson, W. *Lion of the China Sea*, P & O Australia, 1976.

Outpost, the magazine of the Diocese of Victoria.

Padfield, P. *Beneath the House Flag of the P & O*, London, Hutchison, 1982.

Pennell, W. V. *A History of the Hong Kong General Chamber of Commerce, 1861-1961*, Hong Kong, printed by Cathay Press, 1961.

Pryor, E. G. *Hong Kong Book of Records*, Hong Kong, South China Morning Post, 1979.

Ride, L. 'The Antecedents' in B. Harrison (ed.) *University of Hong Kong. The First Fifty Years, 1911-61*, Hong Kong University Press, 1962.

Ride, L. 'The Test of War' in B. Harrison (ed.) *University of Hong Kong. The First Fifty Years, 1911-61*, Hong Kong University Press, 1962.

Sayer, G. R. *Hong Kong, 1862-1919*, Hong Kong University Press, 1975.

Simpson, R. K. M. *Diversions*, Hong Kong, The Hong Kong Daily Press, 1933.

Sincere Diamond Jubilee, 1900-75, Hong Kong, the Sincere Company Ltd, 1975.

Smith, T. 'Compradores of the Hong Kong Bank' in F. King (ed.) *Eastern Banking — Essays in the History of the Hongkong and Shanghai Banking Corporation*, London, Athlone Press, 1983.

Southorn, B. S. *Under the Mosquito Curtain*, Hong Kong, Kelly and Walsh, 1935.

Stericker, J. *A Tear for the Dragon*, London, Arthur Barker, 1958.

Stokes, G. *Queen's College, 1862-1962*, Hong Kong, Queen's College, 1962.

Sung, H. P. 'Legends and Stories of the New Territories', *Hong Kong Naturalist*, 1936.

Thirtieth Anniversary Album of Hong Kong YWCA, 1920-50, Hong Kong, The Association, 1950.

Twenty-Fifth Anniversary, 1900-24, Hong Kong, The Sincere Company Ltd, 1924.

Weiss, K. *Hong Kong Guide*, Hong Kong, The Author, 1953.

Woods, W. *A Brief History of Hong Kong*, Hong Kong, South China Morning Post, 1940.

Woods, W. and Willis, L. 'Mui-tsai in Hong Kong and Malaya', Royal Commission report with minority report by E. Picton–Turberville, London, HMSO, 1937.

Yip, C. L. 'Four Major Buildings in the Architectural History of the Hongkong and Shanghai Banking Corporation' in F. King (ed.) *Eastern Banking. Essays in the History of the Hongkong and Shanghai Banking Corporation*, London, Athlone Press, 1983.

Young Saye, J. L. 'Orchid Hunting on Ma-On Shan', *Hong Kong Naturalist*, 1937.

C.   Dramatis Personae

Marjorie Angus was born in Calcutta and came to Hong Kong in 1924. She was married at St Andrew's Church, Kowloon, in 1934. That same year she left for China, lived in India during the war and returned to Hong Kong in 1949.

Amina and Pat el Arculli's grandfather came out to Hong Kong from India to provision British troops stationed in Kowloon in the 1860s. Arculli Brothers became a thriving business in Hong Kong in the late nineteenth and early twentieth centuries. Their father, Abbas el Arculli, was a solicitor, life president of the Indian Recreation Club and commissioner of the St John's ambulance brigade. The Arculli sisters were raised in Shatin, but after the war moved to Stanley, where Amina still lives. Pat died in 1983.

Dorothy Ballion and Winifred Ward (nées Raven) were raised in the family bungalow at Tsat Tsze Mui in North Point. Their father came out to Hong Kong as an architect for the War Office in 1903 and was joined by their mother in 1913. Dorothy married in Australia during the evacuation and returned to Hong Kong in recent years. She now lives in Repulse Bay. Winifred also returned to Hong Kong with her husband after the war and lives in Shek-O.

Solomon Bard came to Hong Kong from north China in 1934 to attend the Hong Kong University medical school, from which he graduated in 1939. He played the violin in the Hong Kong Philharmonic Orchestra before the war, and co-founded the post-war orchestra, with whom he has appeared as guest conductor. He retired from the post of Hong Kong's director of antiquities in 1983.

Peggy Beard's father, Lennox Godfrey Bird, was a partner in the architectural firm of Palmer and Turner (formerly Bird and Palmer) and from 1919 to 1936 was colonel of the Hong Kong Volunteers. Peggy was born in Hong Kong in 1905, returned to England to finish her schooling and came back to Hong Kong in 1922. She was married at St John's Cathedral in 1928 and subsequently lived in a number of places with her husband Kenneth. She returned to Hong Kong again after forty years' absence in 1973 and now lives in Stanley.

Eugene Chiu was born in China in 1920 and came to Hong Kong as a very young child. He attended Queen's College in the 1930s. He lives in Hong Kong with his wife Rose.

Harry Esmail was born in 1911 in Tin Loc Lane, Wanchai. After attending Diocesan Boys' School, he joined the family business, H.M.H. Esmail and Sons, and worked on the Hong Kong Stock Exchange. Harry led a trade delegation to Japan immediately after the war and retired in 1976.

Eric Himsworth came to Hong Kong as a cadet officer in the government in 1929. He was interned in Stanley camp and became superintendent of Imports and Exports after the war. He has lived on and off in Hong Kong during the last thirty years and, although now retired, makes regular visits to the colony from his home on the Isle of Man.

Colonel Harry Owen Hughes' family has lived in Hong Kong for three generations. His mother's uncle came out in the 1870s as an accountant for Lane, Crawford and later formed his own company, Harry Wicking. Harry's parents came to Hong Kong at the end of the last century. He was born in 1901. He was sent away to school in England in 1909 and returned to join the family firm in 1922. Although he enlisted in the Volunteers, he missed the war in Hong Kong, having been invalided to Australia with TB in early 1941. He worked instead behind enemy lines in China. He returned to Hong Kong after the war and retired in the early 1960s to a thatched cottage in Somerset.

Rosemary Parsons grew up in Hong Kong before the war and attended the Central British School in Kowloon. Her father was head of the naval dockyard. A retired art teacher, she still lives in Hong Kong.

Sin-yu was a sing-song girl in Western district in the 1930s. She became a concubine, bore a child and now lives on her own, in great respectability, in a flat in Mid-levels.

Leslie Ralph was born in 1901. He first came to Hong Kong as an employee of the Union Insurance Company in 1925. He was transferred to a number of places in the East during his career, returning to Hong Kong just before the occupation. Leslie spent the war years interned in Shamshuipo and the post-war years in the Philippines and Japan. He later returned to Hong Kong and retired in 1955 to live in active retirement in Somerset.

Malcolm Swan's father joined Taikoo dockyard from Dumbarton in Scotland. Born at St Paul's Hospital in Causeway Bay in 1923, Malcolm attended Quarry Bay School before going to boarding school in England and returned to Hong Kong again in 1935 to complete his schooling at the Central British School. He joined the government in 1940. As a member of the Volunteers he was interned at Shamshuipo following the occupation but was later transferred to Japan. His brother was killed in Stanley village on Christmas Eve 1941 and his father was interned at Stanley civilian camp. He returned to Hong Kong in 1946 and is now assistant commissioner at the Hong Kong government office in London.

Isa Watson is a member of the Lammert family — her husband still runs Lammert Brothers Auctioneers. The first Lammert came out to Hong Kong from Lithuania in the early 1850s. Her father was born in Hong Kong and met her mother while she was passing through the colony on her way to Japan as a governess. They were married at St John's Cathedral in 1913. Isa was born in Canton but came to Hong Kong as a baby. She escaped evacuation, married Kenneth Watson just before war broke out and spent the years of occupation in Stanley Internment Camp. The Watsons live in Shek-O.

Michael Wright's maternal grandfather arrived in Hong Kong in the late nineteenth century. His father came to Hong Kong as an architect for the government in 1905, met Michael's mother in the cathedral choir and married her in 1910. Michael was born in Hong Kong in 1912, attended the Peak School and left for boarding school in 1921, returning as an architect for the Public Works Department in 1938. As a Volunteer he was incarcerated at Shamshuipo Camp in 1941. He was director of Public Works in Hong Kong from 1963 to 1969. Just before retiring he was asked to run the Hong Kong government office in London and set up the present office in Grafton Street. He now lives in retirement with his wife in London.

Bob Yates was born in Liverpool and came out to Hong Kong as a gunner in the Royal Artillery in 1937. He was stationed on Mount Davis when the Japanese attacked in 1941 and spent the war years in Shamshuipo and in POW camps in Japan. He is a keen student of military history and has revisited Hong Kong twice since the war. He now lives in retirement in London.

ACKNOWLEDGEMENTS

The author and publishers would like to thank the following for permission to reproduce the photographs in this book. The Hong Kong Daily Press; Hong Kong Observer; Hong Kong & Shanghai Hotel Ltd; Hongkong Telegraph; Hongkong & Shanghai Banking Corporation Group Archives; Lane, Crawford Ltd; Mr Alec Hutton-Potts; Mr Bob Yates; Mr Leslie Ralph; Mr Michael Wright; Mr Paul Gillingham; Mrs Marjorie Angus; Mrs Peggy Beard; Mrs Winifred Ward; Overland China Mail; May Collection of Photographs in the Public Records Office of Hong Kong; Royal Hong Kong Police; South China Morning Post.

We are also greatly indebted to the following for permission to reproduce short passages from the works stated:

Alfred A. Knopf (*Margot Fonteyn* by M. Fonteyn), p.60
Annual General Meeting of the Hong Kong Chamber of Commerce, March, 1926 (Governor Clementi's speech), p.7
Athlone Press ('Four Major Buildings in the Architectural History of the Hongkong and Shanghai Banking Corporation' by C. L. Yip in *Eastern Banking. Essays in the History of the Hongkong and Shanghai Banking Corporation*), p.166
BA Dissertation ('The Role of the Hong Kong Woman in Society during the Interwar Period' by E. Lau), p.122
China Mail, p.44
Chinese University of Hong Kong (*Clara Ho Tung. A Hong Kong Lady, Her Family and Her Times* by I. Cheng), p.117
Fanling Times, p.153
Government Sessional Papers: Housing Commission Report, 1935, p.79; Report of Mui-tsai Committee, 1935, p.121; Report on Trade Depression, 1935, p.51
Heinemann (*Mountain of Light* by A. Coates), p.8; (*The Painted Veil* by S. Maugham), p.6
Hong Kong 1938 by W. H. Auden, p. 167
Hong Kong Naturalist. 'Hong Kong Hills' by G. P. S. Heywood, p.152; 'Legends & Stories of the New Territories' by H. P. Sung, p.145; 'The New Territories of Hong Kong' by W. L. Handyside, p.152
Hongkong Telegraph, pp.60, 109, 112
Jonathan Cape (*A Many Splendoured Thing* by Han Suyin), p.17
Kelly and Walsh (*Under the Mosquito Curtain* by B. S. Southorn), p.131
Lane, Crawford Ltd, p.15
London Telegraph, p.44
Longman (*The Go-Between* by L. P. Hartley), p. iv
MA Thesis ('A Study of the 1925-26 Canton-Hong Kong Strike-Boycott' by R. Chung), pp.29, 33, 43
Overland China Mail, pp.25, 55, 171
P & O Australia (*Lion of the China Sea* by W. Olson), p.131
Pan Books (*The Fall of Hong Kong* by T. Carew), p.171
Sheldon Press (*Child Slavery in Hong Kong: The Mui-tsai System* by H. L. Haslewood), p.124
South China Morning Post, pp.1, 7, 29, 32, 37, 51, 53, 60, 92, 94
South China Morning Post (*Eastern Windows – Western Skies* by J. Gittins), p.22
The Crown Colonist, pp.33, 145
The Hong Kong Daily Press, pp.32, 42
The Hong Kong Daily Press (*Diversions* by R. K. M. Simpson), pp.17, 27
Weekly Press, p.92

Every effort has been made to trace copyright, but in the event of any accidental infringement where it has proved untraceable, we shall be pleased to come to a suitable arrangement with the rightful owner.